MODERN MASLOW

TIMELESS WISDOM FOR TODAY'S LEADERS

BRIAN McGEE

MODERN MASLOW
Timeless Wisdom for Today's Leaders

Copyright © 2024 by BRIAN McGEE

Book cover design by Katie Fleming
Interior layout design by Suzanna Chriscoe, Elefont Books

ISBNs:
979-8-89165-197-5 *Paperback*
979-8-89165-198-2 *Hardback*
979-8-89165-199-9 *E-book*

Published by:
Streamline Books
Kansas City, MO
streamlinebookspublishing.com

Dedication

For Lee, Jackson, Will, and Kate.
You've inspired every word.

CONTENTS

INTRODUCTION

December 4, 1994, dawned a cold and wet day in Marlton, NJ, a middle-class suburb of Philadelphia. While many were preparing for the Christmas shopping rush, I had other plans. As a junior defensive back on the Cherokee High School football team, we were about to face off in the state championship game against Washington Township High School, a team ranked by *USA Today* to be in the top ten in the country. No one thought the game would be close—Washington Township had several players committed to play at major colleges the following year, and routinely beat opponents upwards of fifty points.

While far from being the best player on the team, I was good enough to be in the starting lineup on this veteran squad, and had a role to play: don't get beat on a deep pass for a touchdown. On this wet and sloppy day, throwing the football was hard which lessened the threat of a deep pass. However, I was able to make a touchdown-saving tackle in the final seconds of the first half, my biggest contribution of the game. Outside of that play, the players in front of me on defense, the linemen and linebackers, made the other key moments in the game.

The first half of the game ended surprisingly close: 7-6 with our team in the lead. Since we controlled the ball, it kept Washington Township's powerful offense off the field. At halftime, however, our defensive coaches realized an important adjustment could be made: change up the linemen's center of gravity in the wet conditions, preventing them from moving downfield. This ultimately allowed us to keep their speedy players contained.

The adjusted plan worked splendidly. In fact, our opponents *never* scored in the second half. We were able to control the ball on offense, scoring sixteen points and ultimately winning the game 16-6! Our win shocked the country given Washington Township's stature, and the town of Marlton erupted with celebration and pride. For a seventeen-year-old kid, this random day in December was my happiest day.

I learned an important lesson that day: you need to challenge your assumptions and be willing to make adjustments with new information. The world is constantly evolving, and having existential flexibility can make the difference between an exuberant victory or a soul-crushing defeat. Little did I realize I would be revisiting those high school lessons twenty-seven years later.

A global pandemic-induced shutdown forced a kind of halftime for my career. After hard charging for over twenty years, the pandemic forced me, like everyone else, to sit on the sidelines during a tumultuous 2020, giving me the opportunity to take complete inventory of my life and career. What had gone well over the last twenty years? What hadn't? What adjustments did I need to make to ensure a successful and fulfilling next twenty years? Could I chase success and not lose myself in the process?

I had a lot to look back on and several questions to consider. What could I learn from the past to improve my experience in the future? *Better yet, what did "winning" even mean?* The world was moving faster and faster...and I just felt tired. Working hard and investing the time was never an issue for me, but I was starting to see a declining rate of return on my efforts. Trying to be everywhere at once was growing physically exhausting, and keeping up with the constant stream of data and notifications in the information age was like walking into a thirty-foot wave, over and over. Why was my old "formula" for success not working anymore?

Today's leaders have more to grapple with than any previous generation in history. Rapid technological change can render work obsolete in a heartbeat, and decisions must be made faster than ever. Business is quickly becoming globalized, adding complexities in both communication and cultural understanding. The workforce has grown more diverse in demographics, skills, and expectations than ever before, resulting in a higher demand for transparency and accountability.

In addition to those significant changes, business problems are more complex, forcing leaders to deal with these pressures while balancing short-term goals and longer-term sustainability. While the demands of modern-day leadership can be overwhelming, leaders can also make a more significant impact than ever before.

Considering all these changes, I have often sought out books, psychological research, management science journals, and wisdom from today's leaders to solve some of the pandemic-induced questions I was asking. In particular, I was looking for the answers to two key questions: What would be required of today's emerging leaders to succeed in the new world? How would I define success in the future?

Through this journey, I dusted off an often-referenced but rarely-used motivational theory from Abraham Maslow. I first learned about Maslow's hierarchy of needs in a Psychology 101 course my first semester as an undergraduate student at Seton Hall University.

Initial Hierarchy

Abraham Maslow's first attempt at fleshing out the hierarchy of needs was published in "A Theory of Motivation" in the journal *Psychological Review* in 1943.[1] He described the initial conditions in a hierarchy as one need must be met to fulfill the next need. It is important to note that Maslow never intended for this to be a rigid hierarchy. He also never visually depicted the hierarchy in the standard pyramid description we see today, an important detail I will mention several times throughout this book. The pyramid falsely assumes we can check the box on a lower-level need, move on to a higher-level need, and never need to return to the lower level. But this is far from the case. Maslow's needs are fluid, and we can move between the levels as our needs evolve.

Maslow published his simplified hierarchy in 1943, but expanded that definition in the 1960s with additional insight. His original theory was based on the following:

➲ Physiological needs: Breathing, food, water, sleep, homeostasis
➲ Safety needs: Health, personal security, emotional security, financial security
➲ Social belonging needs: Family, friendship, intimacy, trust, acceptance
➲ Esteem needs: Self-respect and respect from others
➲ Self-actualization: Realization of one's full potential

Maslow described the first four levels of the original hierarchy as the "D-needs" or deficiency needs[2], which become all-consuming for the individual to attain them if not met. However, once an individual has met their D-needs, they are no longer conscious and cease to be motivating.

The highest need on the original hierarchy, self-actualization was referred to as a "B-need," or being need. The B-needs refer to the highest levels of consciousness, and once felt, can be motivated to achieve more! We continue to grow as we continue to feed the B-needs.

For many years, Maslow enthusiasts focused solely on self-actualization to "achieve" the summit of human potential. Maslow described self-actualizing people as having some of the following qualities[3]:

⊃ Focusing on reality, not being fake and dishonest
⊃ Centering on problems, focusing on solutions and not on personal shortcomings
⊃ Focusing on the means (how) and not just the ends (outcome)
⊃ Enjoying a balance of solitude and personal relationships
⊃ Having a deep acceptance of self and others
⊃ Exhibiting an unhostile sense of humor, not afraid to show playfulness in self-deprecation
⊃ Having humility and respect toward others
⊃ Showcasing strong moral character and ethics
⊃ Engaging in life with freshness of appreciation, seeing ordinary things with wonder
⊃ Exhibiting creative, inventive, and original ideas
⊃ Enjoying more peak experiences that take you out of yourself, one with life or nature or God

As the years progressed and Maslow's hierarchy was met with success, it's important to note that Maslow himself was restless with the first description of the hierarchy. For many years, the self-actualization tip of the pyramid became the top goal for which many strived. To steal a line from the U.S. Army, the goal was to "be all that you can be." However, Maslow's restlessness recognized that mere self-actualization would lead to a limited life, and much more existed beyond that. Before his death, he would update his hierarchy of needs to build a complete version of his motivational theory.

Most people encounter Maslow's hierarchy of needs in the illustration of a pyramid, which stacks the sequential needs of human behavior on top of each other, peaking in a concept called self-actualization. As an undergraduate, the term self-actualization captivated me twenty-five years ago, and still does to this day. In Maslow's original theory, self-actualization is the culmination of all that one can be, the intersection of achievement and fulfillment. Oh, what a great state to live in! But what does it mean? And how can I get there?

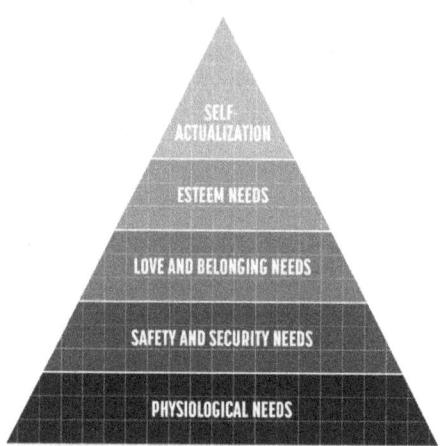

Over the past twenty-five years, I have been enthralled with the concept of self-actualization and how to achieve it. Since the average person spends more than 90,000 hours at their jobs, we have a fantastic opportunity to use this time to optimize who we are and who we can become.[4]

With too much time at home during lockdown, I began to pour over Maslow's research again, considering how the hierarchy could manifest in our careers. Every question I found answers to generated three new questions, keeping me studying at all hours of the morning and night, spiraling down rabbit holes and trying to understand how this wisdom applies to our careers.

My career has had its twists and turns in the medical technology industry, leading sales and marketing teams with novel technology. As I continued to grow and gain outer success with awards and promotions, people came to me for coaching and career advice. I enjoy the process of helping people connect the dots on their own career journey, but after each conversation, I continually found myself wanting more time, dialogue, and the ability to transfer critical information to others.

Maslow's framework became an exciting lens to teach these concepts, as it's a familiar framework that many *think* they understand. After all, plenty of Psychology 101 courses introduced this concept to people who have since tucked it away in the back of their minds. But, as I discovered, many had a limited understanding of the needs themselves, and I had little success in finding anyone who could apply it well, which presented an opportunity.

Maslow's original theory was published in 1943, gaining widespread admiration throughout his life. Despite the significant popularity of his original theory, he was editing his original ideas up until the final years before his death and felt that the work environment was a perfect laboratory for his theory to play out in real, tangible ways.

Despite the apparent opportunities within his edited work, Maslow's theory has sat on a shelf in business books for many decades. Most of this work relates to how businesses can organize themselves around Maslow's theory. However, more books need to be published on how an individual leader can utilize the hierarchy to lead a more prosperous, fulfilling life.

And while a work-life balance and building an identity outside of your career is important, we must recognize that most of us will spend the majority of our waking hours in our jobs. Through that lens, our careers can be a special place to express our best selves, test the limits of our capabilities, and leave a lasting legacy for future generations to benefit.

In this book, you will discover:

➲ **What you learned about Maslow's hierarchy is probably wrong.** We will unveil common misconceptions and new insights into Maslow's famous hierarchy.

➲ **Maslow had a passion for business and found it to be the perfect laboratory for human potential.** His teachings were ahead of their time and can drive effective leadership today.

➲ **Maslow's Magic is in the application, not just the theory.** After each chapter, this book will provide prompts and questions on how to apply Maslow's insights to your career today.

What's in it for Me?

This book offers you a proven framework to pursue career opportunities and accelerate your journey with confidence, whether you're a current or aspiring leader. You will learn the principles of Maslow's framework, what conventional wisdom gets wrong about him, little-known insights from the end of his life, and the magic of applying this wisdom in your career. Wherever you are on your career journey, you can benefit from "Maslow's Magic."

For early career and aspiring leaders, this book is a future roadmap to handling the twists and turns of your leadership journey. My hope is for you to accelerate your journey based on the wisdom of those who went down the road before you.

Mid-career professionals may benefit the most from this book. Mid-career professionals struggle with caring for their personal needs while creating an inclusive and inspiring work environment for their teams. The book's later lessons help develop creativity, beauty, and a deep sense of purpose. These lessons will give you the fortitude to endure modern-day leadership's inevitable peaks, valleys, and plateaus.

Senior leaders can benefit by challenging their assumptions on Maslow and how they are (or are not) applying the framework. **There is a difference between "knowing" Maslow and "applying" Maslow.** At the end of each chapter, questions and prompts will help you apply Maslow's framework immediately. Senior leaders will also benefit from frameworks to show their teams how to drive innovation, create purpose, and tackle emerging trends in the next decade.

What to Expect in This Book

Ultimately, I hope you view this book as one part inspiration, one part education, and one part motivation. The book starts off with Abraham Maslow's little-known insights into Motivational Theory in the workplace and gaps in the current literature for modern leaders until now.

The book will progressively walk through each human need and Maslow's perspective, while providing modern insights to validate his theory. After each chapter, a summary of key themes will help you apply what you learned to your leadership journey immediately.

At the end of each chapter, you'll find a "Maslow Magic" prompt to reflect on how well you fill each need in the hierarchy. The magic isn't just knowing about a particular need but applying it!

You can read *Modern Maslow* in several different ways. You may choose to skim various chapters to gain a general feel for the book and key concepts. However, you are likely experiencing a career scenario where one or a few needs are in hyperdrive. Whatever these needs are, I encourage you to dive deep into those chapters and explore the supporting literature in the Notes section at the end of the book. I always discover my next book to read after a reference in my current book prompts my curiosity. The books, journal articles, websites, etc., can be a treasure trove of insights to help you conquer your leadership challenges and opportunities.

When you finish, you can set it aside on your bookshelf but keep it close. You will continually be challenged with different experiences in your career journey, and you may refer to *Modern Maslow* repeatedly. Since Abraham Maslow's wisdom is timeless, it can be applied in an ongoing basis to provide achievement, fulfillment, and lasting impact on your career.

I thank you for investing money and, most importantly, time to pursue this journey of Maslow's Magic. I hope it will be a fruitful experience you can apply daily. Enjoy the journey. It's time to create your own magic.

CHAPTER 1

MASLOW, THE CAREER COACH

As I hit the campus for my first semester as a college freshman, I had to face many new experiences: adjusting to the demands of a more rigorous and self-directed academic workload. Making new friends from a diverse set of racial, geographic, and economic backgrounds. Working on time management skills in order to balance class, study time, and baseball practice. And, of course, managing the inevitable homesickness from moving away for the first time.

One of my core requirements that fall was an Introduction to Psychology course, which all students were required to take. I had always been interested in how the mind works, and this was my first chance to dive into some of the basics.

It's been said that the two most important days of your life are the day you are born and the day you learn why. As an eighteen-year-old student, I had no clue about that last part, but I really wanted to figure it out. What did it mean to have a successful, meaningful life?

How did I know if my life had value to the world around me? How could this even be defined?

That semester, the work of one man captivated my attention and curiosity. And yes, it turns out he had been grappling with those same questions throughout most of his life.

Abraham Maslow was born in New York in 1908, the son of Russian-Jewish parents who had fled Eastern Europe to escape persecution and secure a better life.[5] However, his family was met with a different form of ethnic prejudice in the United States, as it continued to figure itself out as a melting pot of cultures.

Maslow described himself as neurotic, shy, and lonely during his childhood years, which may have resulted from his early encounters with prejudice. Despite feeling lonely, he made his home in the library, where his love of reading flourished. His timid nature propelled his interest in optimizing the human experience.

A gifted student, Maslow attended Boys High School, one of the top high schools in Brooklyn.[6] He later enrolled in the City College of New York to begin undergraduate education.[7] After graduating from City College, he attended graduate school at the University of Wisconsin and married his wife Bertha. His thesis focused on "learning, retention, and reproduction of verbal material."[8] Despite not being initially proud of the work, it was published in two articles in 1934.

After completing coursework at UW, Maslow continued his research at Columbia University and later at Brooklyn College, Brandeis University, and Columbia. During his time at Columbia, Alfred Adler mentored him, who was an early colleague of Sigmund Freud. Much of psychology, at this time, was focused on the abnormal and ill, focusing more on understanding and explaining human imperfections than anything else. Maslow, however, had a more *positive* mindset. He was intrinsically interested in mental health, human potential, and understanding what humans could become. He called this new focus "Humanistic Psychology."

Humanistic psychology focuses on the positive side of humanity and believes in free will, which differs significantly from behavioral determinism. Some of the core principles of humanistic psychology are described with the following characteristics.[9,10]

- ⮎ A person's present condition is their most significant focus. As a result, humanists emphasize today's experiences instead of examining the past or predicting the future.
- ⮎ Healthy individuals must take personal responsibility for their actions.
- ⮎ Each person is inherently worthy. Despite making mistakes, these actions do not cancel out the value of a person.
- ⮎ Life's ultimate goal is to attain personal growth and understanding. An individual can only be fulfilled through constant self-improvement and self-awareness.
- ⮎ Not all behavior is determined, and free will exists.
- ⮎ Self-actualization (the need for a person to reach maximum potential) is inherently natural.
- ⮎ Each person and each experience is unique, so psychologists should treat each case individually rather than focus on average behavior in group studies.

The Hierarchy Debunked

One of the reasons Maslow's theory grew so popular is its easy explanation of the visual pyramid hierarchy. Remember, though: Maslow never designed a pyramid to describe his motivational theory, and calls out this potential misconception in his paper.[11] "We have spoken so far as if this hierarchy were a fixed order, but actually, it is not nearly as rigid as we may have implied."

Maslow wasn't the first psychologist to develop a human needs theory, but perhaps the visual pyramid clarified the average observer's basic framework.[12] The first account of the pyramid came in 1957 from Keith Davis, an author of a management textbook. In this textbook, Davis depicted a right-angled pyramid rising to a peak with someone raising a flag at the top.

Three years later in 1960, a consulting psychologist named Charles McDermid showcased a pyramid in an article published in *Business Horizons*. This article was titled "How money motivates men." McDermid's pyramid is the one cemented in modern understanding. Despite how Maslow's motivational theory applies to broader concerns of humanity, the first two visual pyramids appearing in a business setting is interesting.

Since Maslow was alive in 1960 and didn't pass away until ten years later, why he didn't challenge this pyramid design remains a mystery. Some researchers believe he felt unappreciated in psychology, even though the management community treated him like a rock star. Recognizing this opportunity for well-deserved appreciation, he either didn't think it too essential or went along with it as it advanced the popularity of his theory.

Regardless of the reasons behind the pyramid's prominence, this visual was never Maslow's intent. Humans can (and do) frequently jump around between various needs as their conditions change. However, the general framework remains relevant since achieving the higher end of the needs spectrum is easier once the lower-end needs are satisfied.

As we evolve throughout our leadership journey with Maslow, our needs will not be met one by one, like advancing levels in a video game. Contrary to popular visual diagrams, it is a process where the lower ends need to be consistently reinforced to move along the journey.

However, once a solid foundation is built on the basic needs, you can focus more on the advanced needs.

One Size Fits All?

One of the other most common criticisms of Maslow's theory is its one-size-fits-all approach to human development. Critics explain that the model caters to the theory's elitist, Western, ethnocentric bias. After all, human experience is not universal throughout the globe.

Critics challenge how Maslow's theory was not proven through rigorous scientific research and used unreliable samples to conclude the study. In some ways, those criticisms are valid.

However, recognizing the impossible nature of actually proving the theory is important. Encompassing the complexity of modern society with its cultural, social, racial, gender, socioeconomic, generational, and regional differences is virtually impossible. Controlling those variables for a conclusive study on human motivation would be equally tough, which is why psychology is so fascinating; it allows us time to ponder and debate these variables.

Regardless of these valid criticisms, Maslow's theory of human motivation provides us with a simple framework as we evolve in our personal lives and careers, serving as a foundation for our development. Particularly in Western societies, plenty of anecdotal evidence aligns with this theory for human motivation, so that through proper discernment and application, we can determine where Maslow's theory fits into our lives.

Maslow recognized some of his work's limitations and even addressed them in his book, *Toward a Psychology of Being*.[13]"There is now emerging over the horizon, a new conception of human sickness and human health, a psychology that I find so thrilling and full of wonderful possibilities that I yield to the temptation to present it publicly even before it is checked or confirmed, and before it can be called reliable scientific knowledge."

What's been most valuable to me—and what makes the most sense—is to look at Maslow's Theory from the lens of what is correct instead of overly fixating on what has not yet been perfected.

The Hierarchy Expanded

Many who learned about Maslow's theory in a college undergraduate program were taught the original hierarchy, which detailed five unique needs: Physiological, Safety/Security, Love/Belonging, Self-Esteem, and Self-Actualization. Self-actualization was the perceived end state for a truly fulfilled life. In fact, one study noted that a Google search of the words "Maslow hierarchy" showed 493 results with only the classic five-level triangle with self-actualization at the top.[14]

The original hierarchy held for nearly three decades. Still, Maslow wrestled with the imperfection of his work while the world celebrated its rigid structure. Shortly before his death, he published an expanded hierarchy of needs, which detailed three new conditions necessary for higher-level beings.

The first two expanded needs expressed the desire for cognitive expansion and pleasing surroundings.[15] The first of the added needs was the Cognitive Needs, which helped open up the need for knowledge, understanding, and creativity in our world.

The second was the Aesthetic Needs and the appreciation of beauty and pleasing surroundings. Aesthetics allow us to find order and balance in a chaotic world. When we stop to appreciate the beauty around us, we grow a little more fulfilled.

The last and most exciting need is transcendence.[16] Transcendence sits as the final destination on Maslow's hierarchy, superseding self-actualization. While self-actualization helped identify the need to maximize your gifts and experiences, Maslow didn't feel like it was enough for a complete life. Instead, the act of transcendence, of creating good in something outside of ourselves, was what really mattered for a fulfilled life.

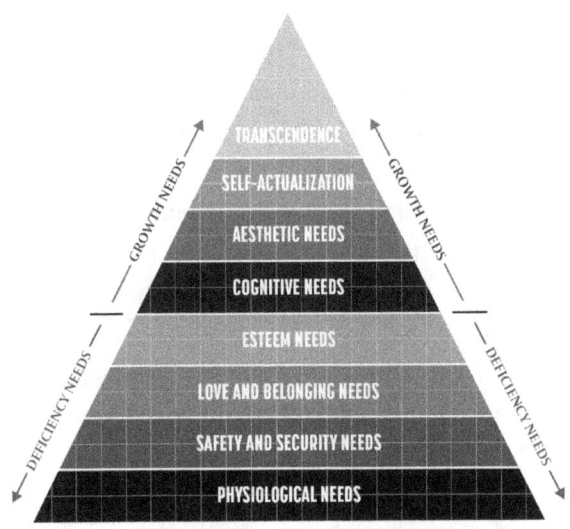

When individuals begin to achieve Transcendence, they are no longer consumed with only the optimization in their lives; instead, they want to make a positive difference in a calling greater than themselves.

Maslow for Business

Despite the high volume of academic publications exploring Maslow's original hierarchy of needs, the application of his work to the business world is significantly more limited. However, through research, we can uncover examples where Maslow tried to connect to our career potential.

In the summer of 1962, Maslow spent time at Non-Linear Systems, a digital voltmeter factory based in San Diego[17]. The leader of NLS, Andrew Kay, used Maslow's book *Motivation and Personality* to inspire a more enlightened workforce. Given an already established foundation of some of Maslow's theories at the company, he decided to see how it played out in a natural work environment firsthand.

Kay noted how his most fulfilled employees worked at the end of the assembly line, where they could see the final product and gain a sense of accomplishment. In response, Kay engineered his company to split into small production teams to self-manage their business, and he even offered an ownership stake with stock options. These changes resulted in both increased productivity and job satisfaction with the NLS employees.

Maslow was fascinated with how his motivational theory could unlock innovation and human potential in the workforce, publishing several of these findings in his first business book: *Eupsychian Management* in 1965.[18] Whether it was the poorly chosen title or his revolutionary ideas, the book failed to take off and only sold 3,000 copies.

Despite Maslow's lack of commercial success in his work, many business pioneers utilized his findings to create a new dimension within their business. Charles Koch of Koch Industries was authorized to reprint *Eupsychian Management* for his senior executives as they built one of the largest private companies in the world. Harley-Davidson utilized Maslow's approaches in their business in the 1980s and 1990s, as well. Other companies, like Whole Foods, Apple, and Pinterest, all point to Maslow's influence on organizational design.

With this renewed business interest in some of Maslow's work, *Maslow on Management* was posthumously published in 1998, almost three decades after his death.[19] This book aimed to collect many of his early thoughts, journal entries, and rough drafts on motivational theory and the workplace. Deborah Stephens edited this work as well as a similarly-themed book titled *The Maslow Business Reader.*[20]

In his foreword for *Maslow on Management*, Warren Bennis describes the book as a collection of musings both "hilariously innocent" and "terrifyingly prescient and penetrating." Maslow confronted some of his time's leading management scholars, including Peter Drucker, Douglas McGregor, Carl Rogers, and Rensis Likert. Peter Drucker claims that Maslow wrote this book to bring McGregor and himself back to Earth.

Maslow thought the industrial workforce to be a perfect testing ground for human potential. "The industrial situation may serve as the new laboratory for the study of the psycho-dynamics, of high human development, of the ideal ecology for the human being." However, the business world, especially in the United States, has evolved considerably since the industrial era. Large factories with long assembly lines making a physical product have been replaced by a service-based economy, filled with a hybrid remote workforce and other open-concept office plans.

Would Maslow's theories still apply in the rapidly evolving 21st century? How can aspiring leaders consider some of these timeless principles to grow their careers?

With this aim in mind, Chip Conley, the former founder and CEO of a boutique hotel chain called Joie de Vivre Hospitality, wrote the exciting book *Peak* in 2007.[21] In his book, Conley attempts to create a new business hierarchy, incorporating many of Maslow's principles for employees, customers, and investors by condensing Maslow's five original hierarchy of needs into three categories: survive, succeed, transform—and build it from the bottom up. Conley applies this methodology to employees, customers, and investors.

Scott Barry Kaufmann released a book, *Transcend*, right in the middle of the global social upheaval of 2020,[22] published like divine intervention when humans were not living their best lives. Kaufmann's work focused on something other than business per se, centering on some of Maslow's final thoughts at the end of his life, in particular the state of transcendence, which supersedes self-actualization as the end state for human flourishing.

As we seek more significant meaning and fulfillment in business, interest in Maslow's work is renewed. We also recognize that the creative engine of the business world can be a force for good, helping solve some of the world's biggest problems and growing into a source of human flourishing.

So, one new set of questions remains: How does an individual business leader progress through Maslow's needs to seek transcendence? How does their career become a combined source of fulfillment, achievement, and good for the world? If the average person spends 90,000 hours at work over the course of their lifetime, how do we make it meaningful for ourselves and the world around us?[23]

The pages ahead explore that journey to combine the principles of psychological research, management science, and leadership wisdom into your career journey. This book is a continual source of inspiration, encouragement, and pragmatism to make your destiny a reality.

Key Themes: Maslow, the Career Coach

- ➲ Abraham Maslow pioneered the humanistic psychology movement. Before Maslow, psychology mainly focused on the abnormal and ill. Maslow flipped the script to focus humanistic psychology on human potential.
- ➲ Despite the success of Maslow's original *Theory of Motivation*, he wrestled with the finality of his framework up to his final years before death.
- ➲ Maslow saw the business world as the perfect laboratory for humanistic psychology, conveying his ideas in *Eupsychian*

Management in the 1960s. Obviously ahead of its time, this title only sold a few thousand copies.

➲ Could the answers to modern-day leadership lie in the psychological wisdom that has been available for more than fifty years?

CHAPTER 2

PHYSIOLOGICAL NEEDS

Put Your Oxygen Mask on First

I don't know if it was the way the Excel spreadsheet lines looked like the beginning of a sword-fighting contest or the fact I could no longer interpret the English language, but something wasn't right. I had just returned from our biggest annual trade show of the year, five action-packed days of meeting with customers, connecting with our global colleagues, and scouting out the competition.

And my mind was toast. I was physically and mentally drained, and even worse, I had to board a flight in 3 days for *another* key trade show in Paris, as this time of year demanded the highest endurance levels. I had a few emails to return and internal communications to draft, but I couldn't complete even the simplest tasks. I felt like only five percent of my mind worked properly, and I didn't know what to do.

The week had been demanding. I'd had early morning breakfast meetings, walked miles on a trade show floor during the day, and attended business meetings at dinner time. I was working hard from 6 a.m. to 10 p.m. daily, with very few breaks and an over-caffeinated nervous system to keep me going. My overwhelming schedule had finally taken its toll.

Not only was I concerned I couldn't put a basic sentence together, but I also had only three days with my family before traveling again. I had three children, ages five, three, and eighteen months, who required a lot of attention. My kids needed their dad, and my wife needed my support and presence. Even if my brain was wiped out, being an emotionally absent father wasn't an option. I needed to push to make them feel like I was present.

My wife, who can spot misalignment in words and actions like an FBI profiler, asked me, "Do you really need to go on this next trip? Is it that important?"

"Of course I do," I replied. Her look communicated her thought perfectly: "Are you sure about that, buddy?" She had always been supportive of my career but would call a spade a spade when she saw it grinding away at my physical and mental health.

Even so, three days later, I boarded the flight to Paris, dreading the trip ahead. My poor diet, lack of sleep and exercise, and inability to tackle my to-do list left me feeling exhausted and guilty.

The City of Love transformed into the City of Fatigue in my mind. I started to think about the uncomfortable airplane seats and getting some rest when it dawned on me: this is an overnight red-eye flight. *Oh good*, I sarcastically said to myself, *I'm going in sleep-deprived and now I get to sleep on a plane overnight*. I knew I was going to keep the Parisian espresso shops busy in the coming days. But the typical overhead announcement interrupted my tired thoughts.

"When in an emergency, please be sure to put on your oxygen mask before helping out any additional passengers."

This statement has always struck me. For one, I couldn't imagine the overriding fear if you were in this position. Secondly, human instinct is to try and help those around you, such as your children who may be flying for the first time.

So why do airplane standards suggest putting your mask on first? If we can't optimally care for ourselves, we can't care for anyone else. Suppose the plane is losing cabin pressure and oxygen. In that case, your perceptions may impact your ability to support your loved ones properly, which places two people at risk.

However, if we can quickly assemble our masks, we can perform with an optimal oxygen level to help others. The oxygen mask analogy creates an interesting parallel for our careers. The "hustle hard" mentality can lead to this same level of oxygen deprivation, literally and figuratively.

So why do we do it? We believe we can cut corners on our health yet still perform at our best in our careers. But nothing is further from the truth. While this mentality may work in the short-term, greater consequences arise long-term, some even life-threatening. Many high achievers put their diets, hydration, and even sleep aside to achieve their "best."

So why do they do it? Because they believe slowing down would be detrimental to their performance. Because going through the drive-thru line at Burger King will be faster than sitting in line for a freshly cut salad. Or because the caffeine from coffee gives us that burst of energy we can't seem to come by with boring, bland water. And we need to send that one additional email at 11 pm instead of having a nightly ritual for healthy sleep.

For those seeking to live on the edge, we can't take our physical health for granted. If we can't show up with our daily A-game or put on our oxygen mask first, we can't be our best for others.

In Maslow's hierarchy, the physiological needs are at the pyramid's base and supersede all other needs. Maslow described the physiological needs as our most basic, like breathing, food, water, sleep, urination/excretion. When these needs go unfulfilled, they consume our minds and any creative functioning in our brains.

The asthmatic patient can describe firsthand the panic they feel when having a breathing attack. Everyone has been "hangry" from not eating during the day. When someone is up all night with a newborn baby, they are sluggish and tired the next morning. And most of us have been on a long car ride with a full bladder and no rest stop bathroom in sight.

When our basic needs are not fulfilled, they consume our being and cognitive energy. Your body is wired for these basic requirements to achieve homeostasis or equilibrium with your functioning. When our basic needs are unmet, our mind and body fixate on achieving them to bring themselves back in order.

Let's explore where physiological needs are pertinent in our leadership journey today.

Sleep

If there is one area many ambitious people cut corners on, it's sleep. For many, wasting seven or eight hours in non-activity mode is a blown opportunity. Why would I spend 1/3 of my life going to bed early when I could stay up a little later to watch the Bachelor or endlessly scroll my phone? After all, you're not accomplishing anything when you're not "doing" anything, correct?

We are obsessed with doing more, reading more, and consuming that last bit of entertainment for the night. We have endless content on Instagram, Netflix, etc., yet we can never shut it down. We think we can get caught up with everything, but we will never get to the bottom of the information barrel. We need to learn to turn it off.

Former Vice President Hubert Humphrey liked to say, "You can't hoot with the owls and then soar with the eagles." Isn't it true? Sleep plays a vital role as a foundational base of health and wellness. Deprivation of sleep leads to forfeiture of performance.

Why do we sleep?

Sleep promotes many functions of a healthy, working body.[24] The impact of sleep is associated with memory function and learning ability, as well as with brain development and cleaning. Sleep can assist in appetite regulation, immune function, aging, mood, well-being, creativity, and enhanced relationships, serving a vital role in the recovery aspect of human existence.

Yet, in modern times, we want to skip our sleep. The hustle-hard mentality and digital connectivity have made it virtually impossible to turn our brains off. Extreme examples of sleep deprivation can have deadly impacts, such as a truck driver getting into an accident by nodding off at the wheel.

But sleep loss has more subtle impacts in the work world, as well. Lack of sleep causes a loss of an estimated $63 billion in the United States each year in the forms of absenteeism and "presenteeism," defined as being present at work but not mentally focused.[25] Employees accomplish less when they are tired, requiring more energy and mental clarity to complete their job effectively.

To operate on an elite level in any domain, you cannot afford to be anything less than your consistent best. We must also recognize that grinding through a sleepy day will not produce your optimal work. The intentional recognition of slowing down to speed up takes discipline.

Understanding the performance gaps of inadequate sleep, several athletes have sworn to its effects as a performance superpower.[26] Tom Brady has been known to go to bed at 8:30 pm every night. Lebron James can sleep up to 12 hours per day when in season. Roger Federer liked to log 11 or 12 hours per night during his tennis career. Spending more time on sleep seems like an extreme commitment to lying horizontal. Still, given the strenuous workloads on their body, sleep optimizes performance during their waking hours.

While it may make sense for elite athletes to optimize sleep given the aggressive exertion on their bodies, would it matter for everyday corporate athletes? The answer is a resounding yes. Many leaders in the field of business recognize the inherent benefits of sleep to their performance[27].

Amazon founder and Executive Chairman Jeff Bezos states he needs at least 8 hours of sleep per night, acknowledging he is more alert and able to think clearly. Microsoft CEO Satya Nadella has also expressed the importance of sleep in his daily routine. Silicon Valley venture capitalist Marc Andreessen recognized that he rarely operated with a full tank when running Netscape in the 1990s, requiring at least 7.5 hours of sleep per night to perform optimally. Even Campbell's CEO Denis Morison understands the personal benefits of sleep to restore energy, rest an active brain, and wake up rejuvenated.

The wearables industry has exploded recently and revealed several truths about sleep for those seeking the edge of an improved workday. These examples include Fitbit, Apple Watch, Aura Ring, and the Whoop band. Many fitness trackers are now working on metrics to analyze sleep. At a minimum, the sleep trackers help you to understand your baseline of a typical night's sleep and its daily effect on your body.

Sleep tracking gives you a general idea of your current sleep state, assessing your progress from week to week. Fitness trackers can measure how you transition in different states of sleep, from light to deep sleep, REM, etc., accumulating the hours spent asleep and HRV (heart rate variability), which can gauge your sleep quality. These trackers are worth the investment in order to start your sleep awareness journey.

While most adults need seven to eight hours of sleep per night, sleep trackers help you fine-tune your needs. After using the Whoop band, many are surprised to see how much they wake up in little spurts throughout the night. Sleep interruptions are common for many people, but these little awake moments can add up to an hour or more throughout the night.

When the COVID shutdown forced me to stop traveling for work, the first thing I recognized was how rested I felt each day. As my sleep patterns grew more consistent without the time zone changes and late business meals, I realized I'd been operating under a major deficit. Curious, I invested in the Whoop band to understand more about my sleep patterns and optimal habits. Emerging from COVID, the habits formed with Whoop help me start my day in a much more restful state, full of energy to tackle the day.

Arianna Huffington wrote a great book titled *The Sleep Revolution*, describing the impact of sleep in our culture and providing recommendations on how to improve our sleep. Huffington's desire to get to the heart of optimal sleep stems from driving herself to exhaustion in her professional life and knowing there had to be a better way.

First, she recommends keeping the bedroom a sleep sanctuary. Many people use their phones, T.V.s, and even work in their bedrooms. By eliminating those options and focusing on just the essentials, you mentally cue your brain that it's time to shut down. You should prepare for sleep as seriously as preparing for a big meeting.

Eating a heavy meal within a few hours of bedtime can alter your sleep performance. Your body will not be able to allow itself to slip into rest mode while actively breaking down the ribeye steak you had with your business colleagues at 9 pm. Give yourself time to eat and digest before bedtime.

Another thing to watch out for is overhydration. While we discuss the importance of hydration for mental performance, over-indulging in fluids a few hours before sleep can also interfere with your sleep. You are prone to visit the bathroom and stumble back to bed, interrupting your sleep patterns. As adults age and sleep interruptions become more common, limiting these interferences to elongate your bedtime is important.

To maximize your sleep, create consistent bed and wake times as well as a "shut down" routine, which signals your body it's time to sleep. Falling asleep is difficult when your mind has been moving at 100 mph and then you try to abruptly fall sleep.

Other sleep hacks include making your sanctuary as dark as possible by using blackout shades and avoiding screens at night. Try using an old-school alarm clock instead of your phone to wake up in the morning. Some researchers are beginning to study the effect of blue light on our brains and our capacity to wind down after downloading information from endless scrolling. The early read on the data: it's not good.

If you choose to read before bed, read fiction over non-fiction, as it tends to turn off your problem-solving mind. Lastly, keep a notepad close. Whether an urgent "to do" popping into your head at 3 am or other random thoughts, quickly write it down and fall asleep knowing you won't forget in the morning.

Most people recognize that a good night's rest is important, and forming this habit can be a performance advantage. After all, war situations often use sleep deprivation to weaken and interrogate prisoners. While most of us (thankfully) are not being held as prisoners of war, why wouldn't we use this vital resource for a performance benefit? While it may seem like a small improvement, the benefits of proper rest will accumulate over time, driving the performance results you seek.

Eat Well

Oh, how we love to eat in Western cultures! Instead of eating to live, many of us live to eat. And why not? An amazing diversity of culinary choices surrounds us. Although food scarcity is a real problem for some Americans and many others worldwide, the percentage of families with food scarcity at some point during the year fell to 10.2 percent in the United Staes in 2021.[28] Declining food insecurity was driven by one of the lowest unemployment rates in modern history pre-COVID-19 pandemic. Other local non-profits, churches, and national organizations like Feeding America are growing in scale and reach. However, a lack of food does not limit the rest of us. Rather, our biggest challenges are limiting the quantity and optimizing the nutritional quality of the food we choose.

Food Awareness

Western societies have difficulty understanding the impact of food on their health. We mindlessly eat foods without determining their impact on our longer-term health. Worse, as information has become more readily available, most people need help understanding what exactly they put into their bodies. We don't address the absolute foundation of Maslow's pyramid because it gets in the way of our daily activities. We push for tasty, readily accessible foods without any understanding of what they do to our bodies. American fast-food culture has exploded over the last few decades, catering to the mindless majority who value convenience over health. And how has that worked out for us?

Obesity is an epidemic in the United States.[29] According to the 2022 Behavioral Risk Factor Surveillance System (BRFSS) data from the CDC, adult obesity rates now exceed 35 percent in 19 states, 30 percent in 41 states, and 25 percent in 49 states. West Virginia and Kentucky have the highest adult obesity rates, over 40 percent. Globally, obesity is now a greater risk than hunger for the first time, according to a 2024 study in *The Lancet*.[30]

In past epidemics, the lack or scarcity of an essential component to life was often at play: the Irish potato famine, the Flint drinking water epidemic, and even the starvation in Ethiopia in the 1980s. Think of the Spanish flu, SARS, MERS, and even COVID-19 when our overall health and well-being were in jeopardy. The epidemic to our security during the terrorist attacks on the U.S. on 9/11. Or the financial system's collapse in 2008, when our basic economic rights seemed compromised. These epidemics occurred when a basic component of human life was taken away.

The obesity epidemic, on the other hand, is an entirely different animal. Some argue that people living in poverty do not have access to healthy choices, or, with a burgeoning mental health crisis, food has become an addiction for people to self-soothe.

But, for most people, the problem lies in *too* many choices. That's correct. We have too much abundance, no control, and our food choices are driving our health down the tubes. Not to mention the extraordinarily high economic cost in a U.S. health system already being taxed.[31] Obesity, which can lead to heart disease, stroke, type 2 diabetes, and cancer, cost the United States $147 billion annually in 2008. By 2030, medical costs associated with obesity are expected to increase by at least $48 billion annually, with the annual loss in economic productivity totaling $390 billion to $580 billion.

We are well aware of the implications of this epidemic, which seemed to hit its fever pitch with the introduction of the movie *Super Size Me* in 2004.[32] For those who have yet to see the movie or understand the premise, filmmaker Morgan Spurlock filmed his life over 30 days eating only food from McDonald's. Over 30 days, he had to eat everything on the menu at least once, and if the cashier asked him, "Do you want to super-size it?," he had to opt for the larger fries and drink.

Throughout this movie, he frequently meets with medical experts to have medical tests performed on his body. Unsurprisingly, over 30 days of McDonald's, his health significantly declined. His physicians warned him to stop the diet because it could have a permanent impact on his health. Spurlock's goal was to bring attention to the dangers of mindlessly eating the current food choices many Americans indulge in.

The results of these poor dietary habits can impact our productivity drastically. Annual medical costs of unhealthy people are $1,429 to $2,741 higher than people of a healthy weight.[33] In addition, a study of over 19,000 workers published in Population Health Management showed a 66 percent loss in productivity in employees with an un-healthy diet.[34] Those figures should make any business leader squirm.

Now, the American way isn't all doom and gloom. Recognition of the rising health and economic impact of poor nutrition in the United States has caused many regulatory bodies to begin to inter-vene. While packaged goods have long had nutritional labeling in the United States, this was not the case for restaurants, but things have started to change. Before federal legislation, New York City and California enacted calorie count laws in restaurants. Congress signed the long-awaited Nutritional Labeling requirements of the Affordable Care Act into law in 2010.[35]

The ACA requirement had several delays in its implementation, so it wasn't formally introduced until 2018. While it only impacts restau-rants with 20 or more locations, it is a significant move in the right direction toward greater consumer awareness of their food choices.

While government regulation is great, it cannot substitute for personal responsibility. We are responsible for our own outcomes in this country. One way to start gaining more awareness of your food choices is to begin a food diary.

During the COVID pandemic, I was paranoid I would gain massive amounts of weight with all the stocked-up "quarantine food" in my pantry, so I decided to track my calories. I used the Fitbit app, which correlated with the device on my wrist, but other services like Apple Watch, Under Armour's MyFitnessPal, the Whoop band, etc., work equally as well. Tracking calories can be a simple exercise. Just log the foods you eat, and the nutritional information is often pre-populated in the app. Most of the time, you don't have to add calorie metrics; it will do it for you.

If digital methods are not your thing, you can also begin with pen and paper to log your food choices in a notebook. Writing these foods down will increase awareness to what you are putting in your body, and you'll see patterns begin to emerge. You may be running to grab a Hershey's bar at 3 pm daily, which could be replaced with a healthier snack.

The wearables market has grown exponentially, poised to have more of an impact in our lives as technology improves. One day we'll all have biometric data on our wrists, which will remotely update our healthcare providers' health status. When any of our vitals get to a dangerous point, they will reach out directly to intervene. Imagine what catching health issues before they strike could do for human longevity and overall care costs.

You can link an activity tracker like Fitbit with a digital calorie count. The Fitbit lets you see how many calories are coming in and out, helping you stay on track for the day. If you want to maintain a stable weight, don't eat more calories than you burn. If you're going to lose weight, a 500-calorie reduction per day (3,500 per week) equals one pound of weight loss. Modern-day technology makes tracking your nutrition easier than ever, making the time and investment in wearable technology worthwhile.

Over time, you may not need to religiously track your calories like you did in the beginning since most people eat similar foods for many of their meals and snacks. But you will get a baseline understanding of your most common food choices to help guide your decisions.

Tracking your calories on an app also holds a hidden motivator. With driven, high performers, the calorie tracking app acts like a scoreboard. You can see how your choices impact your "score" throughout the day, which motivates many people to beat the daily calorie target.

Food Quality

It's no surprise that the average serving size for Americans today is significantly larger than in decades past. The average portion sizes of today's meals almost double our meals 20 years ago. Adults in today's era could take in 500,000 more calories in a given year when it compounds.[36]

For example, the Wall Street Journal recently noted that the average turkey sandwich at a sandwich shop contained about 320 calories in the 1980s. Today, that turkey sandwich has about 820 calories from popular sandwich chains.[37] You're eating over twice the calories in the same sitting, not to mention the increase in sodium, carbohydrates, and added sugars.

This example exposes the rise of take-out eating, the lack of food awareness, and the super-size culture. Unfortunately, some of the bad decisions we've made outside the home manifest inside the house. The first step in changing this pattern is to gain awareness of what you're eating today to establish your baseline caloric intake. From there, you will need to make some behavioral modifications that are not as bad as you think, and here's why.

Many people could benefit by indulging in smaller portions and less food. Shocker, right? But these limitations don't have to be extreme. We don't have to dive into the science about how the body works or the latest understanding of weight loss, but practicing a few manageable tactics to have a sustainable weight will drive your career success. By starting a food diary or utilizing a calorie-tracking app to establish your baseline, you will better understand what to modify.

Portion control or calorie tracking is not a formula for starvation, but we are trying to maintain healthy standards in a world that drives us to make bad choices. You will quickly become accustomed to appropriate portions and food to help you make better decisions. Your goal should be building a sustainable strategy that is easy to execute, not a mad dash to reach an extreme goal weight.

The only guarantees in life are death, taxes, and fad diets. New diets are invented constantly to help sell books, new recipes, and specialty food. Diet trends will continue, but staying rooted in the science and common sense of what is most applicable to your life is important.

A growing body of new trends is popping up, from Weight Watchers to Paleo to Keto. Weight Watchers's points system raises awareness about how much someone is eating, and Paleo and Keto focus on lean proteins and lower-processed foods.

Whatever your diet, massive restrictions on anything will likely not stick over the long haul. The goal of this book isn't to disclose any breakthrough science to give you quick weight loss in a few weeks. Rather, the goal is to provide a simple and sustainable food plan so high performers on the path to Maslow's peak use fuel as energy, not as something that slows them down.

Hydrate

Our bodies need to be well-oiled machines in order to perform our best. Like a race car, we seek the right oil to keep our parts working properly. What is the appropriate "lube" for the high-performance career athlete? You guessed it: water.

Most workers require more water in their daily lives. In one study,[38] the most often cited reasons for not drinking enough water were:

- ➲ I don't feel thirsty.
- ➲ I mostly drink other beverages.
- ➲ I don't have time to get water.
- ➲ I have to pay for bottled water.
- ➲ I drink enough water.
- ➲ I don't like the taste of water at work.
- ➲ I don't trust the water at work.

So how much water should we drink per day? The U.S. National Academies of Sciences, Engineering, and Medicine determined an adequate daily fluid intake is:[39]

- ➲ 15.5 cups (3.7 liters) of fluids a day for men
- ➲ 11.5 cups (2.7 liters) of fluids a day for women

Remember, 20 percent of daily fluid intake usually comes from food while the rest will come from drinks. The age-old advice of eight glasses per day can still apply. However, you may need extra fluids if you exercise in hot weather or work through a cold.

Caffeine

Another significant barrier to proper career hydration is the caffeine-induced culture surrounding us. Starbucks has essentially legalized caffeine addiction, while energy drinks promise a quick jolt when your tank is low. While these drinks provide a short-term boost, they can have significant longer-term consequences. Caffeine can be a catalyst for dehydration, sucking much-needed fluids out of your body.

Per the FDA, the average adult can safely consume 400 mg of caffeine daily.[40] However, many adults respond differently to caffeine, so you will have to look at your own caffeine reaction. Excessive caffeine can cause insomnia, jitters, anxiety, increased heart rate, upset stomach, nausea, and headaches. On days when your excitement level may be heightened, like a big presentation or interview, dialing down the caffeine intake can lessen your nerves.

Even a small degree of dehydration can impact us at work, but proper hydration can improve our productivity, mood, memory, energy level, and mental clarity, all good traits to perform our best!

As we discussed, climbing to Maslow's performance peak isn't isolated to one factor but rather the compounding effects of multiple factors help you operate at your best. Properly focusing on hydration can bring your best self to work and increase productivity. A better mood equals better collaboration with your colleagues. A higher memory level allows you to connect the dots between projects and make better-informed decisions. Increased energy levels bring out your best and rub off on your fellow team members. And lastly, increased clarity helps you make good decisions when the stakes are high.

So, how can we prioritize hydration in our daily lives? Access to good water sources is key. Employers should review their floor plans so thirsty employees don't have to hunt down a glass of water. Also, employers should ensure healthy water sources are abundantly available and not prone to running out on a hot day.

For employees, invest in a temperature-controlled water bottle to always have a full water source next to you at your desired temperature, whether you like your water ice cold or room temperature. For those who don't like the taste of water, electrolyte tablets and mixes can add flavors to your water to spice up your hydration life. Nuun and Liquid IV are two well-known brands, but many others exist. Just make sure that your hydration tablet isn't filled with chemicals or excess sugar which can dilute the benefits of your hydration.

Carrying a water bottle as a consistent accessory (like a wallet, phone, and keys) can help make hydration a better habit. Regardless of how you incorporate proper hydration in your life, the physical and cognitive benefits are real as you ascend Maslow's needs.

Alcohol

No other substance correlates to some of our best and worst moments like alcohol. You've probably seen both effects in yourself or others.

You can bond over great relationships with alcohol or find yourself face down in a toilet after over-imbibing. Alcohol is a perfect example of "everything's great in moderation."

Due to addiction or other health issues, some people are unable to practice moderation. If you feel like you have a problem with alcohol, seek the consultation of a counselor. Sometimes, complete abstinence is the only way, while others may choose to drink alcohol in moderation.

Alcohol is also a known diuretic (like caffeine), sapping your body of the essential fluids it needs to function. As we try to maintain a healthy weight, remember that wine, beer, and liquor can add a significant load of calories into our diet. Calories in your beverages come from two sources: alcohol and sugar. The greater the alcohol concentration and added sugar, the more likely you will put on pounds.

As we discussed with food, water, and caffeine, we can look at alcohol under the guise of a performance mindset. Most rational individuals know that drinking on the job will negatively affect your performance. But we can also acknowledge a different context for alcohol: enjoying it after the workday at home or in a restaurant.

Alcohol can certainly be a catalyst to relax and lower your inhibitions. As you enjoy a happy hour or meal with your colleagues, alcohol can help some people to open up on a more meaningful level. But we have all heard stories of someone making what we like to call a "CLM" or "Career Limiting Move" by overindulging alcohol in a work setting. Alcohol can cause people to behave poorly with others. Even worse, drunk driving puts lives at risk.

With alcohol, be aware of timing. Each alcoholic drink takes approximately one hour to burn off before bed. While alcohol may make you drowsy so you think you fall asleep quicker, your quality of sleep is worse with alcohol in your system. Since we know the importance of sleep, maximizing your restorative sleep is critical to consistent high-performance.

Overindulging the night before a workday can have multiple negative implications. You experience a mental lag even if you're not visibly hung over. You will think less sharply. You may need extra water to cure the dehydration alcohol causes. You may drink more coffee to combat fatigue, which causes further dehydration, anxiety, and general restlessness. To put it frankly, you are not operating at your best.

Like everything else above, using alcohol in moderation can allow you to enjoy the positive effects without hurting your performance. But being mindful of alcohol's impact on the body and potential downfalls on performance (mental, cognitive, and social) if we overindulge is important to remember. For anyone who feels alcohol is hindering their physical performance, mental stamina, and personal relationships, please seek the advice of a counselor. For the rest of us, we must be intentional about alcohol's role in our lives, as it can be like driving through the mud along Maslow's journey.

Move

So, we've discussed the importance of maintaining healthy physiology with what we eat, drink, and how we recover, but high performers also incorporate regular exercise into their schedules.

The attitude of discipline and regularity top performers use to exercise impresses me. Exercise is not a nice-to-have, but a must-have in their day. To fully maximize our physiology, we must prioritize movement in our day. Sure, most of us recognize the physical benefits of exercise, like lower blood pressure, a healthier heart, and a more attractive body, but Ron Friedman of the Harvard Business Review reports social scientists are also beginning to acknowledge the workplace performance benefits of exercise[41].

Regular exercise promotes improved concentration, a sharper memory, faster learning, increased mental stamina, greater creativity, and reduced stress. It can also elevate mood, which is vital when working in team environments and critical interpersonal relationships.

Leeds Metropolitan University completed a study examining the influence of exercise among office workers with access to a gym physically on site.[42] In this study, participants reported visiting the gym helped them manage time more effectively, increased productivity, and improved interactions with their colleagues. They also went home feeling more satisfied at the end of the day.

Exercise has physical and emotional benefits, which can translate into greater work performance. But why do so many people believe they don't have time? The answer is simple: prioritizing exercise is difficult when considering all their other incomplete home and work tasks.

But let's turn that statement on its head. Let's say I told you taking away an activity during the day would cause you to process information more slowly, forget critical work details, increase frustration with your colleagues, and manage your time in a worse manner. Would you sign up for that? Heck no.

Simply put, prioritizing daily exercise, even if it means shortening other activities, is important. The benefits of exercise far outweigh the time spent by making your work more efficient and fulfilling. Wouldn't it be great to experience this satisfaction every day? Try to view exercise as a critical "appointment with yourself" in order to develop the physical and mental capabilities to better perform at your job.

There are many options to get started on a formalized exercise program. Friedman gives three suggestions to help build a routine:

➲ *Identify a physical activity you like:* If you hate running, don't start by spending a grueling 30 minutes on the treadmill. Try something involving movement you enjoy, like tennis, swimming, and even dancing. If you enjoy the activity, you'll likely stick with it.

➲ *Invest in your performance:* Instead of just going through the motions with an activity, try keeping micro goals for yourself. How can you create quantifiable metrics to help you stay on track outside of numbers on a scale? Seeing yourself make progress and gain mastery of new skills will develop confidence and engagement.

➲ *Become part of a group:* Working out in a group gives you the benefit of the social aspects of the gym. And when you have a gym partner dependent on you showing up, you will also find yourself more accountable.

Lastly, variety is the spice of life. Exercise (and life) is boring when you do the same thing repeatedly. Spice it up. Rotate your exercise regimen. Try new and different activities. Never keep two weeks the same, so each day is a novel experience. These rotating experiences will give you a solid foundation of athleticism and may open your eyes to something you enjoy.

Like many people during COVID, I invested in a Peloton bike when my local gym closed. The convenience of exercising at home and eliminating the gym commute was so valuable in my busy schedule. Peloton has also added a diverse platform of exercise choices from bike workouts, strength training, stretching, yoga, pilates, treadmill work, and bootcamp-themed classes. While working out with a group in person has social and motivational benefits , this platform helped me stay consistent with exercise despite my busy schedule.

I've made exercise a daily habit by doing it first thing in the morning. While this commitment does take discipline to go to bed earlier the night before, the overall benefits are immense. I can exercise uninterrupted, as my children are still asleep, and the text/email bombardment has not started for the workday. My mornings begin with more energy, mental clarity, and enthusiasm to take on the day. I've also discovered exercise helps me sleep better at night. When I work hard in the morning, I consciously make better food choices throughout the day because I don't want to destroy the benefits of my workout. My early morning habit has been a catalyst for good choices.

As you begin incorporating exercise into your daily routine, you will quickly realize you are not abandoning other tasks to reach your exercise goals. Rather, you are incorporating regular exercise to accelerate your work performance. We must ensure we bring our best every day in an ever-changing world. For high performance in your career, movement is medicine!

The Great Reset

Abraham Maslow recognized early that our bodies are the temples of the soul. If we don't take care of them, those deficiencies will consume and prevent us from reaching higher realms of being. Much of his writing on physiology focused on extreme hunger or thirst, which could completely preoccupy someone from focusing on anything else. However, in modern times with plenty of choices, poor health decisions can also slow progress toward higher levels of being. Taking care of your body allows you to engage more fully in life, giving you the physical and mental resources to live with elevated meaning.

We need to move beyond looking at our physical health as a "nice-to-have" and start treating it like a "must-have." Do you remember that trip to Paris I was telling you about? Well, on the flight back, I'd finally had enough. Enough of being tired, having low energy, and feeling like I wasn't operating at my highest creative level. I immediately purchased a wearable sleep tracking device, began a regimen of food journaling and early-morning workouts (quickly dropping twelve pounds), and reduced my caffeine intake in order to boost hydration. All of these changes left me feeling more energetic, focused, creative, present, and just plain happier with everyone around me.

Hitting rock bottom forced me to make one clear distinction: My physical health needed to move from nice-to-have to an ***essential*** element of my work and personal life.

Key Themes: Physiology

➲ The impact of sleep is vital to human performance, contributing to memory function and learning ability. Sleep is also associated with brain development and cleaning, appetite regulation, immune function, aging, mood, well-being, creativity, and enhanced relationships.

➲ Proper food choices focused on quality and quantity can significantly impact energy, mood, mental clarity, and cognitive processing speed.

➲ Excessive alcohol and caffeine can negatively affect your hydration and ability to perform. Even a small degree of dehydration can adversely impact us at work. However, proper hydration can improve our productivity, mood, memory, energy level, and mental clarity.

➲ Regular exercise can promote improved concentration, a sharper memory, faster learning, increased mental stamina, greater creativity, and reduced stress, while also elevating mood, which is vital when working in team environments and critical interpersonal relationships.

Maslow Magic: The Magic in the Application

➲ Sleep: Keep a sleep journal for the next two weeks. Each day, note the time you went to bed and time you woke up. Also, note how rested you felt on a scale of one to seven. Notice any trends on your restfulness and focus?

➲ Food journal: Keep a food journal of everything you eat and drink over the next two weeks. With greater awareness, notice any choices slowing down your energy and focus? Are you drinking enough water?

CHAPTER 3

SAFETY AND SECURITY NEEDS

Guaranteed Employment vs. Guaranteed Employability

After ten years working for a large medical technology company, one day I realized my job had grown somewhat monotonous, and I wasn't learning at the same accelerated pace of prior years. I had spent a decade in sales and sales management roles, and I was growing restless and craving new problems to solve.

When my company created a venture to explore a new surgical category for kidney stone treatment, I made the decision to pivot into product management, helping co-lead the most anticipated global product launch in our business unit's history. On paper, this transition looked like a really bad move. I was in a "safe" job in sales management where my reputation was solid, and I had tons of experience to guide me. This new project's success or failure would be visible to everyone inside the company, and the launch plan was still under construction. Also, the research and development team were still working through the final design validation with no predicate device on the market to compare it to. To put it simply, we would be building the airplane as we flew.

My decision held a massive amount of career risk. Our business unit was making a major bet on a new surgical category without having the internal expertise to take on the major established players in our market yet.

Other red flags were obvious in this new role, too. I would have to take a pay cut, lose my team of direct reports, and see my job title fall lower on the org chart. My wife was pregnant with our third child in three years, and the job would require international travel.

Less pay, more travel at a time with more family demands, more uncertainty on product performance, and a *very* public failure if it didn't succeed. What could possibly go wrong?

Nobody would have blamed me for turning the risky opportunity down, but my intuition was insisting something was there. Prior to this opportunity, my career moves had all been calculated and practical. I wasn't known as a huge risk-taker.

So, I did the *opposite* of what conventional wisdom would tell me: I took the job.

After the company announced my new position, I received several confused messages from colleagues. "Congratulations?" "What the heck are you thinking?" My peers were clearly focused on the uncertainty and risk I was taking on. Meanwhile, I couldn't stop obsessing over all the learning opportunities and new problems to solve.

Still, a tiny part of me couldn't help but wonder: *Am I making a huge mistake?*

Maslow on Safety and Security

According to Maslow's original motivational theory, once physiological needs are met, the next focus is our safety or security needs. Observe a child encounter an unknown threat and immediately cower behind their parents. This is a perfect example of our innate need for safety. In adults, this need can manifest through the desire to be safe from wild animals, weather extremes, criminals, tyranny, etc.

In the business world, safety is often fulfilled through features like healthcare benefits, a 401k or pension program, a supportive boss, and job stability. In an article for the *Harvard Business Review*, Amy Gallo suggests several ways to foster psychological safety in the workplace.[43] For one, we should seek out environments with established norms and expectations, so we have a sense of clarity and fairness. These organizations encourage the employee base to communicate and actively listen to one another. Leadership supports their team members by showing appreciation and humility when employees speak up.

Amy Edmundson, the author of *The Fearless Organization*, details the characteristics of a psychologically safe below.[44]

- ➲ If you make a mistake on this team, it is not held against you.
- ➲ Members of this team can bring up problems and tough issues.
- ➲ People on this team try to accept others who are different.
- ➲ It is safe to take a risk on this team.
- ➲ It is easy to ask other members of this team for help.
- ➲ No one on this team would deliberately act in a way that undermines my efforts.
- ➲ When working with my team members, they will value my unique skills and talents.

When an organization values these characteristics, our security needs will be more often met in the workplace. However, buying into the romantic fantasy of "job security" can sometimes trip us up. As technology accelerates growth in the global economy, change is our only guarantee.

I once had a manager tell me he couldn't provide guaranteed employment, but he could provide guaranteed employability. At the time, this comment took me aback, but it makes more sense now. Companies change so frequently, ensuring today's jobs and skill sets will still be relevant tomorrow is difficult, especially in a fast-evolving world. However, if we build the right skills and capabilities along the way, our talents will continue to be desirable to a broad group of potential employers. Thus, we become employable in many different scenarios.

The Roots of Specialization

The traditional career trajectory used to go something like this: You start off bright-eyed and energetic about the world and future possibilities. You show up on time, try to be a good teammate, work hard, and perform well on your assigned tasks. Once you master those tasks and stand out from your peers, you receive a promotion. The process repeats itself until you retire at sixty with a gold watch. You reach your final career milestone by staying with the same company in the same function for forty years or more.

However, this typical job trajectory is certainly not the case anymore. The Bureau of Labor Statistics reports that the average American will have twelve jobs by age fifty-four.[45] TWELVE. Today's career world has obviously shifted from the past. So, how did we get here? And how do we navigate this new world?

Specialization was the modus operandi of the corporate world for centuries, tracing back to Adam Smith, who is widely considered the father of modern capitalism. In *The Wealth of Nations*, Smith devised the theory of specialization.[46] By breaking larger jobs into smaller ones, employees could increase their skills and speed up tasks. Of course, in a simple community, division of labor makes sense. For example, in a village of twenty people, not everyone has the skills or time to make their own candles, so one person who is skilled at making candles becomes the candle maker. He or she knows the most suitable materials to source and how to make production efficient in order to provide the village with a high-quality, low-cost candle.

Specialization continued into the industrial age, as assembly line workers took their places in the factory and executed one rote task over and over. Simplifying who did what sped up the process, producing a better economic result. In the early twentieth century, specialization was the norm.

Now, you might ask, "Doesn't this theory play out in modern times as well?" After all, Malcolm Gladwell wrote about the infamous 10,000-hour rule in his bestselling book, *Outliers*, essentially stating that achieving expert status in a specific skill, like playing the violin, requires at least 10,000 hours of practice.[47] According to Gladwell's logic, specialization seems like a good thing. Except that's not always the case.

Since technology has been the biggest driver of economic growth over the last forty years, we must look at how it has developed and why it relates to specialization. Technology is driving disruption at an unprecedented rate, and Moore's Law offers no better explanation for this disruptive change.

Moore's Law

Moore's Law was named after Gordon Moore, an engineer who started out at Fairfield Semiconductor in the 1960s and later co-founded Intel. Moore pioneered the microprocessor design which determines the speed and capacity of our electronic devices, from laptops to mobile phones. While the semiconductor business developed, he observed an interesting phenomenon. The number of transistors on an integrated circuit doubled approximately every two years as technical designers became increasingly creative. As the number of transistors increase in the same amount of space, our computing power has jumped from mainframe computers and PCs to mobile phones, modern-day gaming, virtual reality, and artificial intelligence.[48]

Following this evolution, our raw computing power has accelerated nearly every business process in exponential ways. This acceleration has forced firms to move faster, causing constant disruption in almost every industry. Today everything is transitory. To survive and thrive according to Maslow's hierarchy, the modern-day corporate athlete needs to prepare for many jobs and industries throughout their career.

Eric "Astro" Teller is the CEO of X, which is Alphabet's (parent company of Google) factory for "moonshot" technology. X is known for inventing breakthrough technologies aimed at large complex problems in the world.[49] Teller has been studying the relationship of technology's pace of change, how humans adapt, and developing "moonshot" technologies to solve systemic issues. In a conversation with New York Times columnist Thomas Friedman, he described this process.[50] Inspired by that conversation, the graph below plots how technology is moving beyond human capacity.

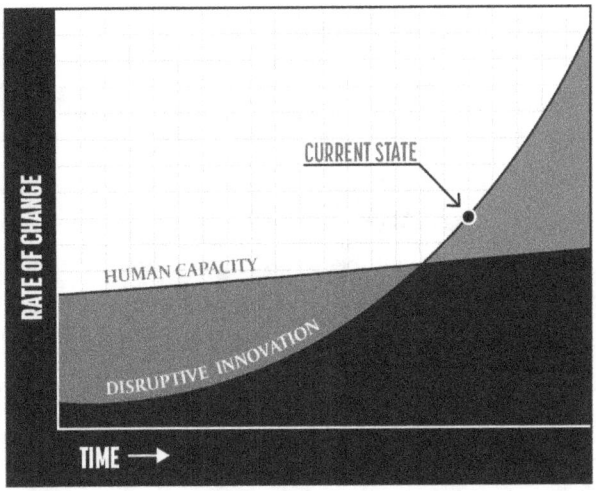

While technology continues to surpass human capacity, specializing in one field or niche no longer guarantees success. Chances are your job will change before you know it or possibly disappear entirely. Lean into change or risk being left behind. Instead of fighting against disruption, high performers must cultivate a curiosity to discover new opportunities.

The Skills of the Future

The idea of frequent, disruptive changes might be challenging because human nature wants to hang on to the certainty of "we have always done it this way." Leaders must lean into technological change to guide their teams towards future opportunities. One example can be found in the looming implications of artificial intelligence. Some leaders will resist AI until they are forced to adopt it, while others are intrigued and already looking for ways to exploit its benefits. Who do you think is going to win in a competitive global market?

Learning how to increase your adaptability will be paramount. Not only will you create new opportunities for yourself, but you will also guide others to habituate themselves to the new, accelerated pace of change.

Technology continues to disrupt modern-day businesses, making specialization in one field or function a thing of the past. Automation and machine learning will begin replacing more and more routine tasks. So, how do we change our modern perspective on career growth in order to survive and thrive? What skills will be critical in this new economy? How do we ensure a machine doesn't make our new skills redundant?

The answers to these questions lie in the three C's: Curiosity, Collaboration, and Communication. Curiosity is the willingness to lean into change with an open, explorative mindset and find a better way. As technology creates more complex challenges, lone wolves won't be able to compare to the problem-solving capacity of a strong collaboration. And as the need for teamwork rises, communication grows even more critical. Future leaders must communicate effectively one-on-one, in larger groups, across cultures and languages, and through technological mediums like email, Zoom, Slack, IM, etc.

While technology promises to increase workplace efficiency, it cannot replace vital human skills necessary to organize the complex world around us.[51] One great example is empathy, which plays a critical role in human interactions by understanding and sharing the emotions of others. Empathy is obviously difficult to build into an automated solution, and machines are not adept at understanding context.

Employers across many industries are now screening for candidates who think critically, communicate clearly, and demonstrate adaptability when faced with change. None of these characteristics are tied to a single job title, but they're all aspects of competency. Regardless of your job title, empathy, context, and adaptable learning will be the most coveted skills in the new economy.

Adaptability may be the new secret sauce for career security. If the only guarantee in our careers is change, how should we approach the jobs in our future?

Expand Your Range, Not Your Specialization

In her book *Lean In*, Sheryl Sandberg describes her career trajectory more like navigating a jungle gym than a career ladder.[52] While most aspiring high performers consider career growth a vertical climb, future leaders will likely take a less direct path forward on their journey. In the new economy, how quickly we develop new skills and capabilities determines our value to organizations.

So, what does the jungle gym look like in practice?

Over the course of your career, you must seek out a broad set of experiences rather than focus on a linear path. Career development may involve changing jobs, companies, industries, etc. You might be tempted to stay on the tried-and-true path because you know what to expect or want to avoid the challenge of learning something new, and while taking the safe route sounds great, does it work?

Andy Ouderkirk, a leader of innovation at the company 3M, wanted to understand the ideal hiring profile for his company, which manufactures products in several fields. So Ouderkirk ran a study examining the backgrounds of elite inventors.[53] The study concluded that inventors with patents in multiple domains had the highest number of patents overall and the greatest commercial impact. This success starkly contrasted the inventors who chose to focus on a specialized domain, which resulted in a more limited commercial impact. While the specialists had a great knack for figuring out technical problems, the generalists were able to transfer their knowledge from one domain to make an impact in another. Their diversity of experience had a cascading effect.

Similarly, music researcher John Sloboda set out to study the backgrounds of exceptional musicians at a British boarding school.[54] To his surprise, Sloboda learned that the students who were classified as "exceptional" at auditions did not come from a musically active family, had practiced their instrument for less time overall, and had taken fewer music lessons. In fact, "exceptional" students were more likely to play three or more instruments, in contrast to those who had more practice time with one instrument. Diversity of expertise trumps specialization once again.

Another example where specialization has become the norm is in youth sports. Youth sports is now a multibillion-dollar business, and many are looking to spot the next Lebron James or Lionel Messi at the age of seven. Kids are under tremendous pressure to specialize in a single sport at earlier and earlier ages. "Top talent" is then funneled into elite club teams and advanced instruction. Training programs have become more and more advanced by introducing practice regimens which overburden the kids' developing bodies. In spite of all of this investment in youth athletes, statistics reveal that specialization isn't the best preparation for most sports or elite performers.

One international meta-analysis examined fifty-one international study reports and 6,096 athletes, including 772 top performers.[55] The analysis revealed that a majority of world-class adult athletes who engaged in more adolescent multisport practice, started their main sport later, and progressed much slower in their main sport than athletes who specialized earlier. Athletes, however, who started their main sport earlier initially showed high levels of excellence but eventually plateaued. So specializing later in their careers allows most elite athletes to attain excellence and sustain their sport longer-term.

In the corporate world, the career profiles of people who end up in the C-suite, the term used to describe the highest-ranking executives in a company, show a similar trend towards diversification. A joint study from the London Business School, Stanford Graduate School of Business, and the University of Notre Dame examined the backgrounds of 506 American CEOs from 233 publicly listed firms.[56] Half of the CEOs came from outside the company they were leading, while CEOs with marketing backgrounds were more likely to have had experiences in other companies and regions. 63.44 percent had worked for three or more employers, and 83 percent had worked in different geographical areas.

Even in the publicly-listed world of healthcare, being a generalist has positive aspects. In recent years, specialists have outpaced the expansion of generalists in the healthcare workforce. During the COVID-19 epidemic, which put a significant strain on the global healthcare system, hospitals and healthcare institutions were understaffed. One paper in the *Journal of Hospital Medicine* discussed the need for specialists to help during COVID, yet these same healthcare providers were out of training in the inpatient setting.[57] In this instance, specialization created a bottleneck of training needs and delayed their ability to add more staff when time was of the essence. The presence of more generalists in the healthcare industry might have helped during this crisis. It's safe to assume that the longer clinicians and healthcare infrastructure were set up to favor specialization, the more it hindered their ability to respond to a deadly virus with speed and agility.

Rajesh Chandy, a professor of marketing at the London Business School, calls career diversification and ingenuity "copy-paste-edit innovation." Creativity is knowing where to copy ideas from, how to edit them, where they apply, and then edit them again. "Innovation is not just a story of dreaming up a new idea," Chandy says. "It's about knowing where to draw inspiration from and how to change things to your own context. And that's where diversity of experience comes in."[58]

A need for deep expertise and specialization still exists in today's world. After all, if a building is on fire, I'd take comfort in the firefighter's knowledge of different flame patterns and smoke scenarios. If someone is negotiating a hostage release, I'd like to know they've been trained in empathy, human connection, and negotiation. Airplane mechanics must also have a critical depth of expertise. But those same airplane mechanics may benefit from understanding how an automobile or a space shuttle works, so they can build transferable skills and increase their creative ability to solve problems.

Many of our jobs today don't present the same level of human risk as an airplane mechanic, firefighter, or hostage negotiator. For most jobs, depth of experience in a specialized domain will help initially, but your ability to add breadth of expertise across many domains will matter even more. Yes, you will be a little uncomfortable at first and sometimes even scared when jumping into the unknown, but the long-term benefits will accelerate your growth and impact. You will reduce the burnout that accompanies the same daily routine, and you will gain transferable skills for multiple fields.

When your existing job begins to feel automatic—i.e., you can perform your tasks on autopilot—it's time to expand your horizons. This expansion could be as simple as taking additional certifications or courses in your current field. Or perhaps jumping into a new industry with a strong long-term trajectory (think healthcare, robotics, artificial intelligence, clean energy, etc.). Or it could mean taking on a radically different role in the same organization.

Curiosity Over Comfort

Back to me: my new role gave me a magnified look at our company-wide operations and helped me develop skills which would pay off further down the road. I worked with R&D, manufacturing, supply chain, regulatory, digital marketing, sales, and our medical education teams—not to mention jumping at the opportunity to travel and connect with commercial leaders on six continents, effectively launching the product in over fifty countries. In my role as product manager, I collaborated with senior leaders worldwide, and they looked to me on how to develop the market for our new product.

Now, great things are done on the backs of teams, not individuals. I had a fantastic teammate and colleague who led the upstream (product development) efforts, while I was partnering with her to lead the downstream (commercialization) process. She knew product management inside and out, mentoring my skill gaps. In return, I helped her with the sales process, sales team psychology, and understanding the complicated maze of hospital purchasing committees.

Our manager was energetic, inspiring, and willing to move mountains to allow the two of us to launch faster. As a former McKinsey consultant, he challenged me to think bigger and more radical than ever before, leaving me invigorated. The three of us differed greatly in our skills, but when we came together, magic seemed to occur. I've never been on such a great team where each team member complemented each other so well. We had a large cross-functional team supporting us in this process, but as the product management team, we were leading the company through a massive change process.

The three of us would have late night text messages about how we could work to drive the launch faster, signing off those threads with "One team, one dream!"

We reinvented the procedure for removing kidney stones, and the product line ultimately became a $150 million+ global business for our company. At the time of this book's release, it has been used in over 500,000 procedures around the world. This first product's success became the foundation for an entire pipeline of future product launches, setting our company apart in the market for years to come.

My experience in that role led to the creation of other roles for me within product management, marketing, and value-based healthcare, eventually landing me a Director of Sales role over a larger organization managing $250 million in yearly sales. If I had not made the choice to make a bold leap of faith over an uncertain product launch, I would never have experienced any of this success at the same accelerated rate.

When I recently asked my new boss why he chose me over the rest of the candidates for the role, he cited my adaptability, strategic thinking, and collaborative style. These skills were honed by working with many different functions across the company and mobilizing change. My crazy leap of faith was exactly the move I needed.

Past employees used to look for guaranteed employment. They worked in one job for their entire career, hoping to eventually collect their retirement benefits and ride off into the sunset, but this guarantee no longer exists. Instead of trying to secure guaranteed employment, we should be developing the qualities that will guarantee our employability. Gaining various expertise will allow you to advance your problem-solving, communication, and collaboration skills and transfer them to numerous environments.

Sara Blakely, founder of Spanx, the billion-dollar women's clothing brand, sums it up well: "The goal is not to be successful. The goal is to be valuable. Once you're valuable, instead of chasing success, it will attract itself to you."[59]

Job security isn't looking for the perfect job at the ideal company under the perfect conditions. All of those things could change in a minute. Job security depends on the valuable, diverse, problem-solving skills you can apply to multiple environments.

Abraham Maslow's original perspective on security focused more on how managers can create an enlightened workforce for their teams, but that was during a period with much less disruptive change. Today, however, leaders need to recognize that seeking stability isn't practical. Career security comes from challenging yourself to build diverse skills and experiences to flex in various problem-solving scenarios. It may sound like a contradiction, but future leaders will remain employable if they *seek out* personal instability by jumping into the unknown to learn new skills.

Key Themes: Security

➲ High-performing teams work in an environment where team members feel psychologically safe and are encouraged to speak up, take risks, and are valued for their intrinsic gifts and talents.

➲ While job specialization served a purpose during the Industrial Revolution, it can limit our ability to take on more complex, dynamic business challenges. Numerous examples in business, sports, education, and music demonstrate the benefits of building a diverse background.

➲ Moore's Law says that technology is driving disruptive change at a pace faster than human adaptability. We must be highly adaptive to respond to new daily challenges.

➲ The most invaluable skills in the new world order will be curiosity, communication, collaboration, and adaptability.

Maslow's Magic: The Magic in the Application

➲ In a few sentences, describe how your current job or industry may be disrupted over the next five years. How will you limit your career if you do not change?

➲ What is one stretch skill you've been looking to develop but have put off? If you were to take action this year, how would it improve your career five years from now? Ten years?

CHAPTER 4

BELONGINGNESS NEEDS
Teamwork Makes the Dream Work

I stood at the gate in Tokyo's Haneda airport, waiting to board a flight for a small city in the South of Japan, Kagoshima. As the Global Product Manager on a new launch, I had the opportunity to travel and launch products on six different continents—a nice little perk of the job. This was my first trip to Japan, and I was eating up the cultural experiences.

When we boarded the flight, I felt like I had arrived in a foreign universe, unlike anything I had experienced before. As you likely know, boarding a flight in the U.S. can feel like a cattle call: every person for themselves, fighting over bin space, stressing over the outlets to charge our devices. Oh, and if we're lucky, we'll get a Diet Coke and a small bag of pretzels.

In Japan, flying is a totally different experience, and I was blown away by how efficient, calm, quiet, and stress-free the whole process was. Passengers were courteous, and they peacefully boarded 100 passengers in about 12 minutes. The more I learned about Japanese culture and the concept of "wa,"—the value placed on social harmony, balance, and cooperation within communities—the more I saw it play out firsthand.

As the plane took off toward the South and I began to observe my surroundings, I had a major revelation: *everyone on this plane is Japanese*, I thought. *The passengers, the pilots, the flight attendants. Except for me.* Now to be clear, everyone was very courteous to each other (including me), but I couldn't stop thinking about how I was so...different.

Maslow and Belongingness

The next motivational need in Maslow's journey is belongingness. During this stage, Maslow described achieving the love (belongingness) needs after fulfilling our physiological and safety needs. "He will hunger for affectionate relations with people in general, namely, for a place in his group, and he will strive with great intensity to achieve this goal," said Maslow in his original Theory of Motivation.[60]

In our professional lives, we all want to belong to a group with shared values since relationships are central to our lives. Humans are pack animals, not designed to live on our own. This phenomenon dates back to the early times of men and women, where tribes formed for the safety and well-being of the group.

But on its basic level, humans were meant to be a part of a group, to feel a sense of love, belonging, and connectedness with each other. If a prehistoric man or woman could not provide value to the group, they might be shunned by their cohort to fend for their food and safety. If a man or woman could not make themselves appealing to the opposite sex, they would not reproduce and extend their bloodlines. In short, unattachment to a group caused many negative risks.

We also see the breakdown of this critical need for belonging in today's political culture. While different tribes (i.e., political parties) will band together to reinforce their values, we are seeing the broader culture disintegrate as we stop listening to one another and become stuck in our group identities.

The same sense of belonging is deeply felt in today's work culture. Whether seeking a new organization to evolve your career or looking to build a team to thrive in today's fast-paced world, Maslow's theory of belonging is critical in your workplace evolution.

What Got You Here Won't Get You There

At this stage of your career journey, you've begun to showcase your value with diversified skills and the potential to lead others. But moving from an individual contributor to a team leader creates significant change as you are no longer controlling the final results, your team is.

And this is a difficult transition for many top performers to make as they attempt to achieve the same results through others. It was so much easier when you could just do it yourself! This section will discuss the importance of culture, values, recruiting, team formation, and execution. By creating a strong foundation of belongingness within the group, the conditions are right for individuals to do their best work. After all, the "TEAM" acronym is "Together Everyone Achieves More."

But before we start on those meaty topics, let's first anchor ourselves into what NOT to do as a first-time leader. Some skills that made you a superstar individual contributor will hold you back as a team leader.

Marshall Goldsmith, an author and management consultant, has extensively researched some of the key traits holding back dynamite individual contributors towards becoming effective leaders. In his work, Goldsmith outlines the bad practices that a leader commonly does to impede their impact.[61]

Some of Goldsmith's findings include:

- ⮑ Winning too much: The need to win at all costs and in all situations.
- ⮑ Adding too much value: The overwhelming desire to add our two cents to every discussion.
- ⮑ Making destructive comments: The needless sarcasm and cutting remarks we think make us witty.
- ⮑ Telling the world how smart we are: The need to show people we're smarter than they think we are.
- ⮑ Speaking when angry: Using emotional volatility as a management tool.
- ⮑ Withholding information: The refusal to share information to maintain an advantage over others.
- ⮑ Failing to give proper recognition: The inability to give praise and reward.
- ⮑ Claiming undeserving credit: The most annoying way to overestimate our contribution to success.
- ⮑ Making excuses: We need to reposition our annoying behavior as a permanent fixture so people can excuse us.
- ⮑ Refusing to express regret: The inability to take responsibility for our actions, admit we're wrong, or recognize how our actions affect others.
- ⮑ Not listening: The most passive-aggressive form of disrespect for colleagues.
- ⮑ An excessive need to be "me": Exalting our faults as virtues simply because they're who we are.

These qualities will not build a healthy sense of belonging in any team environment. Instead, exhibiting any of these will destroy communication, team trust, appropriate risk-taking and new innovation. As new leaders and recovering individual contributors, we need to overcome any of those traits that may have fueled our relentless passion to achieve more. Sometimes, it makes sense to start on what NOT to do.

Culture and Values

If an organization's structure is the hardware, then culture is the software. Culture is the personality of an organization, the sum of an organization's values, traditions, beliefs, interactions, behaviors, and attitudes.[62] In a competitive marketplace, culture can make or break your team.

Why does culture matter? After all, beliefs and values don't increase profit, right? Not so fast! Culture is foundational to your strategy because it attracts talent, drives engagement and retention, impacts happiness and satisfaction, and affects performance. Culture is the connective tissue on how work gets done.

We could write an entire book on culture, its importance, and strategies to improve it in your work setting. While adding a few ping pong tables and virtual happy hours may seem an easy rubber stamp for culture, being intentional about what cultural values are important for your team is essential. If you take care of your employees, they will care for your customers.

If you care for your customers, they will care for your revenue. If you take care of your revenue, it will take care of your shareholders. If your shareholders see improved returns, they will continue to invest in the business.

And the positive cycle continues.

When most people define culture, the first instinct is a feel-good spirit to make coming to work an enjoyable activity. Let's make work less miserable! However, it's much deeper than that. Culture is a magnet for talent, builds fulfillment in your work's purpose, creates trust, and drives high performance.

Billionaire investor Warren Buffett likes to discuss the difference between an inner and outer scorecard.[63] The world wants to judge us on the outer scorecard: the company's revenue or stock price, or individual metrics like income, job title, or number of Instagram followers. While they may be data points to judge small aspects of the business, the outer scoreboard only captures some of what is needed for sustainable, durable success. But what does matter is the inner scorecard.

The inner scorecard refers to your own personal values that provide you with peace and comfort. Many people frequently over-subscribe to the outer scoreboard or are judged by other people's opinions, which can cause poor decisions and questionable ethics. When faced with a tough ethical decision, Buffett challenges his managers to consider the "newspaper" test. If the local newspaper published the manager's decision for the world to see, would they be proud of it? If their decision passes that test, it's ok. If it's too close to call, it's a bad ethical choice.

Your values will underpin your behavior with your team, customers, and other stakeholders and serve as the foundation of your culture. Your culture becomes the company's operating system, your decision-making lens. Over time, the quality of your choices influences your performance.

Attracting Top Talent

When I graduated college, I remember looking at the "Help Wanted" section in the local paper for jobs, but fortunately, recruiting talent for your team has evolved considerably. In place of want ads, companies placed their jobs on websites and job boards, expecting, "if you post it, they will come." As job seekers, we all remember this experience. You see an intriguing job, take an hour to fill out the questions, then—poof—your application is sent to the black hole of Human Resources, most likely to never get a response. It was an imperfect process for both the prospective employee and the employer.

However, technology has accelerated the hiring process, and you can no longer wait on a stack of qualified resumes to hire the perfect candidate.

The talent competition is at an unprecedented level. When writing this book, the United States had one of the lowest unemployment rates in the last 50 years. Top talent often has multiple options. Many recruiters have told me that if you find a good candidate, you'd better move quickly because that candidate will have multiple offers. So, how do we recruit top talent for our organizations when the stakes are so high? We need to attract talent when we are not hiring.

What is a talent attractor? Simply put, this is someone to whom people are naturally drawn. They have the right values, charisma, energy, and technical competency to develop great people around them. Instead of waiting for job openings on their team and going through the standard interview process, they are always recruiting. Instead of waiting for top talent to sell themselves in an interview process, they are pursuing top talent and selling their organization. Before an opportunity even manifests.

How do they do it? Well, they utilize their organic networks, looking for potential talent to join their team and make a difference. In many ways, they start the interview process before a job opening has even begun.

Social networks are a great opportunity to connect with new talent and grow your brand as a leader. While there are many platforms to use, LinkedIn is the most popular platform for business leaders and prospective employees. LinkedIn is a forum where people present the professional version of themselves compared to other social networks. While other platforms are great for connection, LinkedIn provides a way to post intriguing and inspiring content related to your field. Your friends and followers become attracted to your ideas, priorities, and communication style, and as you post relevant content each week, you will develop even more of a following. Depending on your career and audience, Instagram, Facebook, Twitter may also be acceptable formats.

But why would I make time to talk to new candidates when I don't even have a job opening on my team? I have so many other fires to put out! What a waste of time.

Yes, however, recruiting great talent is hard work and a constant process. But do you know what else is hard? Having mediocre talent and having a low-performing team. The question is: Which hard scenario would you prefer?

Future Learning Potential

Some of the most coveted skills in the new economy will be emotional intelligence, complex decision-making, and learning adaptability. In my experience, one of the best tools to develop emotional intelligence is the 360 review. A 360 review occurs when a broad group of stakeholders provides anonymous feedback on your strengths and weaknesses as a teammate. If you use the data as a tool to improve instead of a personal indictment, it can grow your emotional intelligence to effectively work with others.

You can hone your complex problem solving and learning adaptability by building a diverse set of career experiences, as explained in the previous chapter. You will develop the skills to sift through ambiguous data sets and quickly make decisions because you have practiced jumping into unique scenarios in the past.

In my experience as a commercial leader in the medical technology field, I have had both hiring successes and failures. I have hired a candidate I thought was a slam dunk for a role only to watch them quickly unravel in the new job. I've also hired a few dark horses despite their imperfections, and saw them achieve massive amounts of success. However, from past experience, I have developed a simple acronym to discern who would succeed in a rapidly changing environment. It was time to PISTL-UP!

PISTL-UP is a general framework for evaluating candidates for your organization's future roles. They stand for:

P: Presence
I: Intelligence (and curiosity)
S: Success history
T: Thought process
L: Leadership

However, in my experience, this acronym needs two more aspects:

U: (Sense of) urgency
P: Passion

Let's take a moment to explore each aspect of the acronym.

Presence is tricky, and I am not referring to judging a book by its cover, but first impressions matter. Many of our judgments occur within the first few minutes of meeting someone, and we immediately ask ourselves questions. Does this person radiate a solid presence? Did they show up on time for the interview? Are they professional or rude? How do they make me feel when I'm around them? Have they done their homework on my company and position or did they show up unprepared? A person's presence can add calm to your workplace or cause disruption, even if you can't explain why. In an environment where work colleagues, external business partners, and customers interact with your people, presence is critically important.

The next component is intelligence, which is pretty straightforward. Does this individual have the technical know-how to do the job? Do they have the social intelligence to work well within a team? While we can always inspire or encourage growth in our employees, you can only execute at a high level if the inherent skills already exist. To put it bluntly: You can't make chicken salad from chicken scraps.

Success history is an important aspect as well. A person's success history consists of more than just having executed well in a previous job. We need to ask if they have a knack for "figuring it out"? This aspect looks at how well someone adapts to building successful strategies in diverse settings. The world is rapidly changing, and this individual must adjust.

The next critical component of onboarding is thought process, which is the ability to break down complex challenges and reassemble them into creative solutions. The more routine the task, the more likely it will be automated, but the ability to provide context to scenarios and connect the dots can't be automated. How well does this individual break down a problem and try to solve it systematically?

One of the final components of successful hires is leadership. This isn't leadership in the old-school, dogmatic sense of the word, or the stereotypical high performer who is a charismatic extrovert. Leadership, simply put, is the ability to influence others positively. Contrary to popular opinion, leadership comes in all shapes and sizes. How does this individual better others around them? Leaders can be found everywhere in the organization and with any title.

Now, for a good chunk of my hiring career, I stopped at those competencies when looking to hire someone new. I thought this acronym gave me a 360 perspective on all aspects necessary for a top performer.

Depending on your team or employee's needs, you would weigh each competency differently, but it is a good framework. However,

I have yet to find an experienced leader with a perfect hiring record, because we all make mistakes. I also saw individuals with impressive resumes, credentials, and skill sets who sometimes fell short of less talented coworkers. So, what else could be missing?

And then it hit me—while competencies and experiences are great, the driving engine of high performers is in their hearts. High performers have a passionate, healthy obsession with their work and operate with a strong urgency to get things done. What can be done today gets done today.

Grit: The X-Factor for High Performance

The driving X-factor emerging in consistent top performers is passion and perseverance over an extended period. Career success is never a linear, vertical journey, but quite the opposite. It can zig, zag, plateau, and even appear to decline in small chunks as you navigate your career. Top talent shows the resilience to see this chaotic journey through. The enjoyment of pursuing their goal outweighs the work and time they dedicate to achieve it. High performers are loaded with GRIT. Grit is a popular term originally coined by author and researcher Angelia Duckworth.

In her research Duckworth describes our natural talent bias in today's world, where we value talent as a snapshot of time compared to the capacity to learn over time through hard work.[64] We believe talent trumps hard work, evident in how we initially overlook the late bloomer in school, sports, arts, etc. These individuals often struggle early but persevere later.

So, what sets these individuals apart?

First, they possess a high intrinsic motivation for what they do instead of being solely motivated through extrinsic measures. With extrinsic motivation, we are rewarded by the outward signs of success like awards, promotions, raises, or fancy job titles. Intrinsically motivated people love to dive into the work itself.

This person is the quintessential "gym rat" who would rather shoot free throws in basketball than hang out with friends on a Friday. Or the scientist who spends their weekends in the lab to solve the impossible problem. Or the product manager who obsesses over market models to find the tiny crack of opportunity for their new product launch.

Child prodigies also reveal some of these same traits. Ellen Winner, a psychologist from Boston College, has studied these child prodigies to understand what makes these children elite.

Outside of innate talent, a common denominator in these kids was a *rage to master.*[65] High performers who can sustain this advantage over time have an extreme curiosity and intense need to discover. The intrinsic motivation comes from the inside. They have joy in figuring it out and won't stop until they get it.

Of course, this isn't to say that promotions, awards, and raises don't matter; they certainly do. But they are not the primary motivator for these individuals. Top performers have a love of the process itself.

Identifying the wrong talent can begin early. Schools routinely reward students for being talented at one moment, but they may not be life-long learners. If children are more willing to take a risk on something, they are more likely to see their capabilities evolve at the same time. Conversely, if the students feel like they are constantly being judged, they may be unwilling to extend outside their comfort zone.

We make similar mistakes in the workforce. While holding a baseline of talent or experience on your team is important, we must understand how a new candidate's passions and processes will transfer over to the new job, which will matter more for their lifetime performance.

In Duckworth's work, she describes two critical formulas for success:

Talent x Effort = Skill
Skill x Effort = Achievement

We all enter the world with natural talents and tendencies, and working on these initial talents will improve your overall skills. Effort isn't just going through the motions but deliberately practicing our intended skill. In Malcolm Gladwell's *Outliers*, he describes 10,000 hours of practice as a key component to elite performers in many fields (the arts, science, sports, etc.).[66] Many readers over-generalized this comment to conclude that practice was deliberately going after the same activity over and over.

This concept of deliberate practice was based on psychologist Anders Ericsson's work, who originally wrote the 10,000 hours concept in his work "The Role of Deliberate Practice in the Acquisition of Expert Performance," published in 1993.[67] While investing the time is important, we also need to use that time intentionally. Instead of just going through the motions, we need feedback to see what is and isn't working, which will enable us to make continual adjustments. In short, deliberate practice requires effort.

Then, once we have developed our skills, we must continually improve in order to achieve. So, while talent and skill are one part of the equation, effort shows up in every stage and compounds over time.

As a talent attractor, we must understand the key skills of the future (emotional intelligence, learning adaptability, and complex decision-making) can be found in several different profiles. While depth and breadth of experience matter, we must recognize the heartbeat of the future employee. Your ideal talent archetype will have a growth mindset with grit, passion, and perseverance over a longer period.

Forming-Storming-Norming

When we think of a high-performing team, what image comes to mind? It could be the Chicago Bulls of the 1990s, with great stars like Michael Jordan, Scottie Pippen, and Dennis Rodman, among others.

Or perhaps it was the U.S. Special Forces team, a group of elite soldiers, who raided Osama bin Laden's compound in the middle of the night? Or could it be the early employees of a technology conglomerate like Google, Facebook, or Microsoft, whose creative energies and insane work hours brought about game-changing technology for today's world?

Were these teams built with a cohesive group of individuals destined for success from day one? Hardly.

All high-performing teams go through a process to figure out their inner DNA in order to achieve high success. While talent is important, how the team works and functions as a unit is even more important.

To sort out these complex dynamics between humans and high-performing groups, American psychologist Bruce Tuckman published a landmark paper in 1965 detailing the systematic steps high-performing groups go through to perform at a high level. His work, which describes the steps—Forming, Storming, Norming, and Performing—has become a model for successful team development[68]. He later added a final step, Adjourning, to his work.

When a new team forms, teammates experience an early buzz and excitement about the new venture. It could be the critical nature of the project the group is working on. Or, it sparks the curiosity and intrigue of the team because it's a challenging problem to solve. Or, maybe, it's just the opportunity to work with new colleagues and learn different working styles.

Frequently, these forming events can have a high level of pomp and circumstance, with fancy kick-off meetings, keynotes from business leaders, and the usual company merchandise with inspirational slogans. Optimism abounds, and the group is ready to take on the world!

But then, reality intervenes. This group has a new problem to solve with new people in new roles, which introduces uncertainty about the plan and subsequent responsibility. Our teams then fall into the next stage—Storming. This stage happens to all high-performing teams as they evolve into one unit. I used the aforementioned Chicago Bulls example as a good start. The 1990s Bulls teams gave the illusion that everyone was bought in and aligned to coach Phil Jackson's vision, but the reality was far from it. After watching the award-winning documentary, *The Last Dance*, you quickly learned the team was far from perfect. If Twitter existed in the 1990s, I can only imagine what team drama could have originated from Dennis Rodman!

As people assemble into new roles and with new leadership, an air of uncertainty can be uncomfortable for the team. Leadership may ask star employees in other units to play a supporting role on their new team. Or ask others to stretch into unknown assignments with career risks at stake. Some may question if the team can even achieve its desired outcome. The biggest mistake leaders can make during this stage is giving up on their people too early. Although, it's natural to have some doubts when the path isn't clear, we must be patient with our teams and allow them time to process their questions and uncertainty.

Strong leaders embrace the ambiguity, as being unsettled will drive the team to seek optimal ways to work together.

Just under the surface of this unease is often a breakthrough idea.

During the norming stage, the dust settles on the newly formed teams. Individuals are adapting to their new roles, establishing new working relationships, and beginning to work more harmoniously. However, despite the more orderly working climate, the new unit may still lack meaningful progress on their intended goals, which is simply part of the process. The team needs to establish consistent routines before seeing success, and the leader's role during this part of the journey is to keep the team focused on their goal.

As the team establishes positive working styles and norms, the cohesive behavior will begin producing visible positive outcomes to both the team and the organization. Now is the time for the team to celebrate some of the smaller milestones being met, which can fuel the fire of their motivation. The team has worked through its earlier challenges and emerged as a stronger group on the other side.

Lastly, in 1975 Tuckman added a final stage of team development after doing additional research on his model called the adjourning stage, or as some also call it, the "Deforming and Mourning" stage. While we might want to believe that teams work through their challenges early to succeed into infinity, this is far from reality. Star performers will move on to other assignments with increased responsibility. Sometimes leadership only puts teams together for a time-bound project which, when completed, will disperse the team to their next assignments. Sometimes the organization assigns individuals to "figure it out" in a different business unit to understand strategy and long-term success.

As employees leave the original team, are they leaving behind the systems and norms so the next person can pick up where they left off? Or is the entire group's success dependent on the tribal knowledge of the founders? Does the team recruit with similar values and commitment to excellence?

Some employees who value certainty in their roles may begin to feel uncertain again as they transition to their next assignment. For these employees, acknowledge their reaction is natural, just as it was at the start of the project. By clearly supporting these employees during transition, they will be more confident to take on their next assignment.

Effective Teams

The mechanics of working in a group are becoming more important as the workforce evolves to automate basic processes and utilize teams for complex tasks. A great team can make amazing breakthroughs, but a dysfunctional team can be hell on earth for its members. As a leader, your role is to create team dynamics so members can perform at their best.

Google once hypothesized that managers were a necessary evil and could be an additional layer of bureaucracy slowing down great work. They commissioned an internal study to prove the hypothesis that managers didn't matter and the manager's quality didn't impact their team's performance.[69] The study defined manager quality on performance ratings and feedback from Google's annual employee survey. The results were shocking and actually proved the *opposite* of the original hypothesis.

Managers did matter, and their team's happiness and success depended on it. The Google researchers conducted double-blind interviews with the best and worst managers to find examples of their different actions. Their results revealed that the best manager...

➲ Is a good coach
➲ Empowers the team and does not micromanage
➲ Creates an inclusive team environment, showing concern for success and well-being
➲ Is productive and results-oriented
➲ Is a good communicator-listens and shares information
➲ Supports career development and discusses performance
➲ Has a clear vision and strategy for the team
➲ Has key technical skills to help advise the team
➲ Collaborates across the company (Google)
➲ Is a strong decision-maker

Leaders dictate the team's values, culture, and operating system, and leaders who exude those positive characteristics are on their way to creating a healthy team dynamic, setting the tone from the top down.

To take their study further, Google looked at what qualities set apart the stronger working teams from the lower performing groups.[70] Google studied 250 attributes of 180+ active teams and conducted over 200 interviews with their employees to uncover a great team's secret sauce. They learned that the team's talent was less impactful on performance than how the team members interacted, structured their work, and viewed their contributions.

Five Key Themes Emerged from the Google Study:

- ⊃ *Psychological Safety:* Team members need to know they can take risks and communicate what's on their minds. Can they make a bold suggestion for the team without feeling insecure or embarrassed? Will leaders recognize mistakes as part of the process, or will they publicly ridicule failures? Judgment in the building phase will destroy creativity. Team members need to know they can show up as themselves, and the group is open-minded to their input.
- ⊃ *Dependability:* Can they count on each other to complete high-quality work on time? Due to the interconnectedness of project work, punctuality is key. Teams need to know that when a colleague says they will do something, they deliver on it.
- ⊃ *Structure and clarity:* Are goals, roles, and execution plans clear? This structure becomes very apparent in the complex, ever-changing world of ambiguous problem-solving. A leader's mission is to help clarify what the team is trying to accomplish, who will do what, and what timeline they are under.
- ⊃ *Meaning of work:* A difference exists between a job and a meaningful career. While we may not love all aspects of our role, we recognize its overriding meaning in our lives.
- ⊃ *Impact of work:* Team members must know their work matters. Whether the contribution is big or small, managers must communicate to their colleagues how their work matters to the world around them.

Develop a Sense of Belonging

Humans are tribal beings with a basic need to belong in a group. We desire connection, significance, and a human support structure during various seasons of life. Building great teams will be the hallmark of any strong leader as we ascend the career hierarchy.

Jim Rohn had a famous quote: "You become the average of the five people you spend the most time with." The same quote holds true for a team. As iron sharpens iron, a strong group will rub off on each other and elevate each other's game.

The same goes for talent and values. Legendary UCLA men's basketball coach John Wooden famously said, "You'll never outperform your inner circle." You need to build a strong team with high standards of performance and culture.

Leaders come from many backgrounds with vastly different working styles. However, high-performing leaders share consistent traits when creating a sense of belonging in their teams; they are clear about their values, which form the backbone of a strong culture. The culture can serve as an effective tool to attract the diversified talent necessary for success.

All teams will evolve, from Forming to Adjourning, and an effective leader will navigate the path for them. Google reminds us that great teams have strong leaders who provide a haven for employees to do their best work.

Enlightenment at 30,000 Feet

As a white guy in corporate America, I usually didn't have to look very far to find someone who resembles me. While I always appreciated diverse teams, my flight in Japan was the first time I actually *felt* what it was like to be different, the odd man out. And wow, what a profound feeling. I thought about being the outlier the entire trip—a feeling both heavy and enlightening. For me, I only had two hours of feeling different, but others feel different their entire careers.

This experience struck me on how some people might feel in a traditional, corporate American setting. For example, if their gender, racial, or religious identities make them feel like outliers to their group setting, I can see how that may cause additional stress. Or what if someone with a disability worries about their limitations holding them back from other's *perceptions* of their career talent? The list goes on and on.

That moment on the plane shaped my leadership philosophy, renewing my focus on belongingness and unity in the workplace. I knew if I was to truly mobilize the best talent from all sources, everyone needed to *feel* like they belonged. I couldn't afford for anyone to hold back—and I didn't want them to feel like they had to, either. My approach? If you have great ideas and can work in a team setting, you have a spot on this team. Our differences bring unique perspectives to accomplish great things in our work.

Now, the aforementioned examples just describe visible diversity. Keep in mind, diversity also lies under the surface. How do different working styles, skill sets, and divergent career profiles all come together to bring the best out of everyone? Does the introvert feel valued and included in a team of extroverts? Everyone should feel comfortable in showing up as they are, and the best leaders prioritize inclusivity and belonging in their environments to make that a reality.

When team members feel like they belong, they are more likely to feel comfortable sharing their opinions and ideas, leading to greater collaboration and innovation. Additionally, a culture of belongingness can boost morale and reduce turnover, as team members are more likely to stay with a company that values and respects them. Ultimately, a culture of belongingness can lead to increased creativity, greater job satisfaction, and a more positive work environment for everyone.

Abraham Maslow recognized the importance of group identity, and feeling accepted, valued, and connected to others with similar pursuits. Isolation can squash our ability to ascend Maslow's Motivational Theory, depriving us of reaching our transcendent impact. If we are serious about reaching our full potential as a leader, building a culture of belonging is paramount to our success.

On the United States dollar bill, you can read a Latin phrase titled, "E Pluribus Unum," which translates to, "Out of many, one." As leaders, we must cultivate a feeling of belonging for EVERY employee.

Key Themes: Belonging

➲ Culture is the sum of an organization's values, traditions, beliefs, interactions, behaviors, and attitudes. In a competitive marketplace, this can make or break your team. Culture is the ultimate talent attractor.

➲ One practical framework for evaluating talent is the PISTL-UP approach: Presence, Intelligence, Success History, Thought Process, Leadership, Sense of Urgency, and Passion for the job.

➲ Grit, defined as passion and perseverance over an extended period of time, is a key driver of long-term achievement.

➲ An internal study on successful teams in Google revealed five key components to make or break a group. Those include psychological safety, dependability, structure and clarity, meaning of work, and impact of work.

Maslow Magic: The Magic in the Application

➲ What traits made you successful as an individual contributor and now hold you back as a leader? In what ways do they slow you down?

➲ What five themes are most important in your culture? Is your team even aware of them today? Where are you living up to your cultural expectations, and where are you falling short? What future skillset is going to be paramount for your team to succeed in the next five years?

CHAPTER 5

ESTEEM NEEDS
The Dark Wilderness
of Vulnerability

"Ten minutes to stage time," the production assistant reminded me as we were about to go live. The day had come; I was in Arizona for our big kickoff of a major new product line, our big release to the U.S. sales force. Hundreds of people were in the crowd, excited to see what was in store for the business and this expansion.

Taking a giant leap into product management after a long commitment to sales was a huge challenge. It was a high-profile project, and I was in over my head. Our Division President at the time said it well: "Brian, we usually give newer people low-risk assignments when they come to product management for the first time. They get a chance to cut their teeth on something small, and if they screw up, it's not that big of a deal. But this is the most anticipated product launch we have ever had in this business." No pressure, right?

"Five minutes to stage time." While I was excited, a jittery nervousness was beginning to take hold of my physiological state. Our entire U.S. sales team was present, and I was also beginning to see members of our R&D teams and company executives file in. Our international leaders had flown in to learn more about this exciting product line to take back to their home countries. We also had a few well-known expert physicians present who would speak after me concerning their interest in this new product category.

At our yearly kickoff meeting, we were planning our launch presentations to make a big splash with sales and marketing. I would need to step forward to lead my former peers on this high-profile project that our business unit's success would hinge upon. Everything was about to come full circle.

"Two minutes to stage time." Panic mode set in. I wear a heart rate monitor, and my beats per minute were two times my resting heart rate. I had never experience this level of nerves before a presentation. *Will I be able to pull this off?* I wondered. I had been chosen to lead this major product launch, and I may not even be able to get the words out of my mouth.

"One minute to stage time." Are we *really* going to do this? I fought the urge to run behind a cactus and get lost in the Arizona terrain. I had taken a bold leap into co-leading this major product launch, making this my most visible leadership job. A million thoughts raced through my mind: *Am I up to the challenge? Will I deliver on the immense expectations?*

The lights in the room darkened as the stage lights grew brighter. The booming announcer's voice said, "Now coming to the stage, Global Product Manager, Brian McGee." They played a walk up song I can't even remember because my heart was racing so fast. Taking a deep breath, I made my way to the stage.

Maslow on Esteem

When thinking of the word "Esteem," the next Maslow need, I can't help but think of the Stuart Smalley sketches from Saturday Night Live in the 1990s.[71] Al Franken played the character of Stuart Smalley, which satirized the modern self-help movement of the time. As part of the show, Stuart would look in the mirror and give a personal affirmation…"I'm good enough. I'm smart enough, and doggone it, people like me."

Smalley, a sensitive character with clear esteem issues, was trying to use the catchphrases of the times to will his way to a happier life. It was both funny and sad at the same time.

Of course, this SNL sketch isn't exactly what Abraham Maslow had in mind with this next need on the hierarchy. But, to understand the importance of esteem within today's career development framework, we should take it from the man himself:

> All people in our society (with few pathological exceptions) have a need or desire for a stable, firmly based, (usually) high evaluation of themselves, for self-respect, or self-esteem, and for the esteem of others. By firmly based self-esteem, we mean that which is soundly based upon real capacity, achievement and respect from others.
>
> These needs may be classified into two subsidiary sets. These are, first, the desire for strength, for achievement, for adequacy, for confidence in the face of the world and for independence and freedom. Secondly, we have what we may call the desire for reputation or prestige (defining it as respect or esteem from other people), recognition, attention, importance or appreciation.[72]

The implications of esteem are significant. Maslow said, "Satisfaction of the self-esteem need leads to feelings of self-confidence, worth, strength, capability, and adequacy of being useful and necessary in the world. But, thwarting of these needs produces feelings of inferiority, of weakness and of helplessness."

Maslow's esteem accelerates human potential because striving for recognition, respect, and achievement is fundamental to our nature. This need is closely linked with our sense of self-worth and confidence, which are crucial to achieving personal growth and fulfillment. By fulfilling our esteem needs, we can unlock our full potential to become the best version of ourselves. Whether through work or relationships, we all have a deep desire to be valued and appreciated. Maslow's esteem need recognizes and validates that aspect of our humanity.

Viewing esteem through two lenses is essential. How do we think about ourselves, and how do we negotiate the world around us that may not always be kind? Do we approach our failures with constructive curiosity, or do we lambaste ourselves with brutal criticism? Waiting for others to validate everything is also a recipe for disaster, a significant constrictor to human flourishing.

Man in the Arena

A year after President Theodore Roosevelt left the presidential office, he spent a year traveling, hunting, and giving speeches in cities like Cairo, Berlin, Naples, and Oxford. During this time, Roosevelt noticed the abundance of cynics who would look down upon the men trying to make the world a better place. He was quoted as saying, "A cynical habit of thought and speech, a readiness to criticize work which the critic himself never tries to perform, an intellectual aloofness which will not accept contact with life's realities—all these are marks not of superiority but of weakness."[73]

Out of these observations, he delivered one of the most inspirational speeches in Paris in 1910. Originally titled "Citizenship in a Republic", it later gained prominence with the title "The Man in the Arena":

> It is not the critic who counts; not the man who points out how the strong man stumbles, or where the doer of deeds could have done them better. The credit belongs to the man who is actually in the arena, whose face is marred by dust and sweat and blood; who strives valiantly; who errs, who comes short again and again, because there is no effort without error and shortcoming; but who does actually strive to do the deeds; who knows great enthusiasms, the great devotions; who spends himself in a worthy cause; who at the best knows in the end the triumph of high achievement, and who at the worst, if he fails, at least fails while daring greatly, so that his place shall never be with those cold and timid souls who neither know victory nor defeat.

In this great quote, Roosevelt is dictating that the man or woman who fails while trying to "dare greatly" at solving some of the world's biggest problems is of greater virtue than the cynics who are too afraid to enter the arena at all. What a profound message! Giving too much power to the critics will prevent you from doing your best work.

Your critic may be a vocal heckler, office gossip, or even a judgmental parent or boss. In the modern era, the critic can be a social media troll who hides behind their keyboard. Or even worse, the critic could be yourself.

As we navigate our leadership journey, we must confront the critic head-on—the critic within ourselves and the critic in the world.

Confronting the Inner Critic

When developing this book, I stumbled across the research of Brené Brown, a researcher at the University of Houston. She holds the Huffington Foundation Endowed Chair position at the University, and is a visiting professor in management at the University of Texas at Austin McCombs School of Business. For over two decades, Brown has been writing and researching the topics of courage, vulnerability, shame, and empathy.[74] She is a bestselling author and a great speaker on the stage, with viral TED Talks receiving over 50 million views. I know what you're thinking—wow, shame and vulnerability sounds like a party! Who's bringing the chips?

All kidding aside, when I discovered her work, it unlocked an intense curiosity to learn more about how our self-talk can hold us back and how we can break free from those self-imposed limitations.

Through Brown's work, we discover that people with inherent self-worth experience greater love and belonging. If they can show up as they are, they feel worthy of love and belonging, which is why the previous step in team building is so essential. An inclusive team accepting each other for who they are, will foster an environment where team members feel a greater sense of worthiness.

However, shame and guilt can creep in on the worthiness prevention team.[75] Brown has a simple expression which details the difference between shame and guilt: Guilt says that I have done something bad. Shame says that I am a bad person.

Though uncomfortable, guilt can remind us we are not living up to our expectations and can strive to do better. On the other hand, shame tells us we will never be good enough. Shame likes to get in our heads with questions like, "Who do you think you are?" It's negative self-talk at its worst.

Negative self-talk can lead to imposter syndrome, a condition coined by the psychologists Suzanne Imes and Paulina Rose Clance.[76]

Imposter syndrome is a term for an inspiring performer who cannot internalize and accept their success. They feel it's up to fate, luck, or connections, not their fundamental skills and talents that brought them to where they are. It's intellectual self-doubt at its worst, as we have the recurring loop of "I hope they don't find me out" in our heads. Shame can show up in different ways across race, gender, age, experience, etc.

Shame is an epidemic in the U.S. driving violence, addiction, depression, aggression, and suicide. Brown details that in order to combat this shame, the U.S. is the most obese, medicated, and addicted society it's ever been. At best, shame prevents us from doing our best work. At worst, it can mean death in our bodies and souls.

As humans, we are imperfect beings. Waiting to get into the proverbial arena of life until you are bulletproof and perfect will not happen. You will either sit on the sidelines or accept your imperfections and get in the game.

Individuals balancing achievement and esteem do not stake their personal identity on their outcomes or skills. They place their identity on their values and pursuit of excellence, how they show up daily for themselves and others. Note the word "pursuit" and not guaranteed excellence. Sheer excellence may not be attainable, but attitude, preparation, and effort all further the pursuit of excellence. Our Founding Fathers did not ensure happiness in the United States. Still, they did proclaim that all beings were entitled to "life, liberty, and the *pursuit* of happiness." Happiness and success are not within our final control.

But how we show up is.

Esteem is a complicated topic for people who have experienced success in the early stages of their careers. Being told you are a great student, athlete, musician, or employee can distort your viewpoint to believe that those achievements define who you are.

This distortion is what makes it so hard for high achievers to build their identity around self and not outcomes. It's not to say that results don't matter, but they are not the final definition of who we are.

So how do we correct this lens of shame and obsessing over our imperfections? Of the self-doubt creeping in and telling us we are not enough? The answer:

Vulnerability.

For many, vulnerability sounds like a weakness, but in reality, it's the most accurate measurement of courage. Vulnerability requires you to accept your imperfections and not be held back by them.

Vulnerability requires you to not lie to yourself about your imperfections, but work to improve every day. Vulnerability recognizes where we are presently but throws itself at the improvement process. Vulnerability is about pursuing mastery, knowing the process will take time and involve heartache, but we do it anyway because our purpose is much greater than the discomfort.

Brené Brown joked in one of her TED talks that her work has become very popular with larger organizations. She noted one phone call from a business leader who wanted her to come in to speak to their employees, but wanted her to avoid the words shame and vulnerability. Why, she asked? This business leader thought it would hold them back from the necessary work of creativity, innovation, and change.

Brown thought this was funny because the truth is the opposite; vulnerability *is* the pathway to creativity, innovation, and change, if only we could drop our old perceptions and see the obvious.

Vulnerability is the courage to be imperfect, the compassion to be kind to yourself and others when you don't measure up to your own expectations. And it builds a connection with ourselves and others built on authenticity. It allows us to let go of who we "should" be.

And be just fine with who we are.

There are no prerequisites for worthiness, no external outcome to achieve; your humanity defines your worthiness, not your achievements.

Letting go of the stress of artificial standards opens the door to creativity, innovation, and change.

To fully embrace vulnerability, we need to accept ourselves unconditionally. We must also abandon the idea that to be "enough," we must fit societal standards. We must reject the notion that we must prove ourselves and please others. And lastly, we need to believe we deserve love and belonging simply because we are.

Once we embrace ourselves as we are, we gain the courage to move forward in an uncertain world with changing dynamics. We believe we will figure it out as we go.

Carol Dweck, a psychologist at Stanford University, notes that high performers who sustain a competitive advantage over time exude a "growth mindset." The brain is a muscle that can be trained. In her book, "Mindset," Dweck details the impacts of a growth mindset versus a fixed mindset.[77]

Individuals with a fixed mindset feel like their talents are set in stone. The fixed mindset always judges where they are in the moment, and avoids difficulties. After all, if they don't try, they can't fail! The fixed mindset believes that failure will make them a loser forever.

In the fixed mindset, talent is king and cannot be undone. The fixed mindset thinks their brand is at stake depending on the outcome of any challenge. They make excuses for why they are the way they are. In extreme cases, they cheat because they recognize their limitations. They don't try to make themselves any better because, in their eyes, it's a useless waste of time.

In contrast, individuals with a growth mindset hold a completely different perspective. They recognize their current talents and skills are just a snapshot in time and can be trained. Children with a growth mindset understand that the more problems they can solve, the smarter they grow. Instead of seeking approval for where they are today, they seek to show progress. They lean into challenges and relish them.

Growth-minded individuals don't condemn themselves for mistakes, but recognize they are necessary to grow. They use adversity and negative feedback as mere data points to self-correct and try a different path next time. They take satisfaction in pushing themselves to their limits. The individual with a growth mindset is constantly looking to refine and adjust, and they're not afraid to take on an "impossible" challenge because they don't define themselves by the outcome.

The heart and mind are muscles that need to be trained. As a growth mindset becomes the norm and we continually push our capacity, we will undoubtedly build success and self-confidence. Dr. Michael Gervais, a sport and performance psychologist who works with many elite athletes worldwide, defines confidence as the ability to say to yourself, "I can do hard things."

High performers have a higher tolerance for discomfort and can thrive under pressure. They seek challenging circumstances to push their edges and see what they can do.

Living in this discomfort is the norm for high achievers. Jill Ellis, the former U.S. women's national soccer team's head coach, said it best. "Other teams visit pressure. We LIVE in the pressure."[78]

Duke University women's basketball coach Kara Lawson had a great spin on it.[79] Lawson describes top performers as people who handle "hard better." Although top performers make it look easy, it never really is.

They learn how to handle the hard, then raise their standards. Once they achieve one goal, they elevate their standards with something harder. They are never comfortable but are always on a path to "handle hard better."

As your resilience improves, you gain confidence knowing you've been in the fire before but came out the other side. And even thrived. After all, you have survived 100 percent of your hardest days! So what do you tell yourself when you face a new obstacle? You've got this!

NBA basketball coach Doc Rivers shares one of his philosophies: "Pressure is a Privilege."[80] Leaders thrive under pressure. When the stakes are high, they rise to the challenge. The mere fact of stepping into the arena and competing gives you an excellent opportunity. Pressure is a privilege.

But shame can prevent us from discovering ourselves. By having empathy for who we are and being vulnerable to truth, we open ourselves up to self-acceptance. This vulnerability is the launching pad to showcase our growth mindset and take on tough challenges. As we develop more and more examples of wins in challenging scenarios, we can look at ourselves in the mirror and confidently say, "I can do hard things."

This journey of self-acceptance is a long and difficult one that will ultimately unlock your soul's energy. Are you going to be your coach, saying, "You've got this!" Or will the inner critic raise its ugly head and ask who the heck you think you are?

Taming the Haters

"Care what other people think and you will always
be their prisoner." -Lao Tzu

When seeking out a new team or organization for employment, you need to understand their values and cultural operating system in advance.

Workplace environment is not something you want to leave to chance. Even though culture and values are less objective than industry, job title, salary, etc., they're just as important in the long run, ultimately defining your fulfillment, support, and comfort in the workplace.

By working to find an organization or company that aligns with your values and cultural standards, you can reduce the number of challenges you will experience in a toxic culture. You will be that much further ahead in doing your best work as your best self.

Even in healthy organizations, it's human nature to wonder what others are thinking of you. You've heard of YOLO—You Only Live Once. And you've probably heard of FOMO—Fear of Missing Out. But as sport and performance psychologist Michael Gervais says, we have a new four-letter acronym to describe a concerning modern-day behavior, FOPO—Fear of Other People's Opinions.[81]

Gervais works individually with world record holders, Olympians, internationally acclaimed artists and musicians, MVPs from every major sport, and Fortune 100 CEOs. Gervais co-founded the company Compete to Create, with Seattle Seahawks coach Pete Carroll. The company focuses on bringing the skills and tools of a high-performance mindset to sports and business organizations. Compete to Create works with clients such as Microsoft, AT&T, and Amazon to enhance culture and individual performance through high-performance mindset training.

FOPO is the irrational and unproductive obsession with what others think about us. As we've discussed, we have ancient tribal brains hard-wired for approval; we want to be accepted, liked, and loved, making it hard to stand on our own.

In ancient times, approval was a matter of life and death. Not being accepted by the tribe could mean banishment, being left alone to seek food, shelter, and protection from saber-toothed tigers.

Unless you are a zookeeper, most of us aren't worrying about steering clear of saber-toothed tigers during the day. But the "tiger" can take several different forms. Your personal "tiger" could be the opinion of your boss, work colleagues, or old high school buddies. Or, perhaps you aren't sure your new love interest loves you back. And, in the modern era of social media, faceless trolls can be brutal in their feedback and comments.

But do these external forces present the same life-or-death scenario as the caveman experienced? Usually not.

However, our brains are still hard-wired with these ancient scenarios even though they present themselves in today's modern era with much less physical risk. We can get the same heart-pounding, sweaty hands, adrenaline-induced fight-or-flight response as if we were encountering the tiger.

So how do we overcome this response?

First, recognize the thoughts and feelings and be aware of them, and let yourself off the hook for feeling what you do. Many of us can be highly critical of our feelings, even though it's a hard-wired response. So, take a breath and drop the judgment.

Once you've acknowledged the feeling, incorporate positive self-talk. As we discussed with your internal criticisms, remind yourself that "I can do hard things." Remind yourself of past successes to draw confidence for the next obstacle. Remind yourself you prepared for this interview. That you are a great public speaker and can move an audience. That you are a hard worker with creative solutions to complex challenges. Whatever your self-talk, you can draw upon your past wins to anchor your mind in a better place.

In addition, developing a "personal philosophy" can be beneficial. Per Gervais, this is a word or phrase expressing your basic beliefs and values. When coming up with a personal philosophy, Gervais writes that you can ask yourself the following questions:

➲ When I'm at my best, what beliefs lie beneath my thoughts and actions?
➲ What people demonstrate characteristics and qualities that align with mine?
➲ What are those qualities?
➲ What are your favorite quotes? What are your favorite words?

Pete Carroll, head coach of the NFL's Seattle Seahawks, has a simple personal philosophy of "Always Compete," which doesn't necessarily mean competing against a foe but rather a philosophy of working hard to be better than the day before.

Gervais also coached an executive who was driven by the struggles of his immigrant parents. He felt accountable to take advantage of the opportunities they gave him and make the family name proud. His philosophy was "Walk worthy." Whatever your philosophy, this motto can be a great self-talk anchor when you feel FOPO coming on.

For successful people, criticism is inevitable. As Aristotle said, "To avoid criticism, say nothing, do nothing, be nothing." Standing out is not easy, and you will become a target because of your unique nature and courage to put yourself out there.

Tim Ferris has a unique collection of thoughts regarding handling the haters. I'm sure Tim's success has attracted his share of critics, but through it all, he's managed an impressive resume of accomplishments, including being an early-stage technology investor to companies like Uber, Facebook, and Shopify. He's also written five #1 bestselling books, and his podcast was the first business/interview podcast to exceed 100 million downloads.[82]

Tim has assembled seven great principles for dealing with the haters, which are inevitable on the path to success.[83]

- ⮑ It doesn't matter how many people don't get it. What matters is how many people do.
- ⮑ 10 percent of people will find a way to take anything personally. Expect it.
- ⮑ "Trying to get everyone to like you is a sign of mediocrity." -Colin Powell
- ⮑ "If you are really effective at what you do, 95 percent of the things said about you will be negative." -Sports Agent, Scott Boras
- ⮑ "If you want to improve, be content to be thought foolish and stupid." -Epictetus
- ⮑ "Living well is the best revenge." -George Herbert

➲ Keep calm and carry on.

But why do critics emerge in the first place? There could be several reasons why you or your work may be criticized. And it doesn't all need to be bad.

Some critics legitimately want the best for you. Sometimes your work does fall short, and they are pointing out ways to refine and improve the project.

Or, the critic may fear you are setting yourself up for failure and wants to stop a bad idea in its tracks. But we need to discern whether the critic holds a real educated viewpoint or if we should respectfully dismiss their opinions.

Others fear your success because it exposes a weakness in themselves. You may be tired of your physical appearance and energy levels and commit to a healthier lifestyle. Your unhealthy friends may worry this will expose more of their insecurities. Or you may decide to take a bold career risk. Your risk-averse friends may worry about your success because it could propel you into a new circle of higher-achieving friends.

And some people, well, are just there to annoy. Martha Stout is an author, psychologist, and clinical instructor in psychiatry at Harvard Medical School. She wrote the book *The Sociopath Next Door*, which is a frightening title, to say the least. Stout estimates that four percent of the global population are sociopaths, making that 1 in every 25 people with whom you come into contact.[84] These people have no conscience, sense of right or wrong, empathy, or ability to understand emotion.

So, when faced with criticism, we need to see if people fall into one of four categories.

First, is it honest feedback we need to improve our work? Or is it a well-meaning but uninformed person misguided in their feedback?

Is it someone your success will threaten because it will make them feel worse about themselves? Or is it just a jerk?

Regardless of who delivers the criticism, the path to success requires us to endure the heat. With the growth of team-based projects and workplace collaboration, you invite more opinions of your work. And with the increase of social media, any clown can hide behind their keyboard and fire off an abrasive critique.

Tim Urban wrote a great post on his blog, *Wait But Why*, titled "Taming the Mammoth. Why You Should Stop Caring What Other People Think."[85] Tim offers some common-sense wisdom to handling the haters.

Tim's blog perfectly depicts the battle between The Great Mammoth and The Authentic Voice. The Mammoth is your social survival instinct, which obsesses about everyone else's thoughts. The Authentic Voice is, you guessed it, who you truly are and what you can become.

Criticism destroys The Mammoth. The Mammoth thinks that everyone is talking about them, worrying that everyone will talk about them if they do this risky or weird thing.

The truth is people don't think about us as much as we think they do. How disappointing! Since most people stare at their phones all day and spend 99.9 percent of their mental energy obsessing about their own lives, they simply don't have time to worry about you.

Judgy people don't matter. They are highly mammoth-controlled individuals who attract other mammoth-controlled people. They are boring, predictable people who are jealous if you're different..

Unsurprisingly, people gravitate more to the Authentic Voice (AV) because it's real, honest, and unafraid to be itself. The AVs lead, while the mammoths only follow. The AV recognizes that even if the mammoth crowd doesn't approve of them, it rarely has any consequences in their life. It's not worth their time or energy to pay attention their disapproval, because after all, the Authentic Voice has more important things to do.

We can't be surprised when we encounter critics; instead, we should embrace the critics because they are necessary to become our best.

From Panic to Joy

In Arizona, I opened my presentation with a few painstakingly prepared statements. Though the room looked dark from the dimmed lights, I could feel the energy pulsing in the room. I could make out a few friendly faces of my old sales colleagues in the front of the crowd. We locked eyes and smiled at each other. One gave me a wink and a thumbs up.

To this day I don't know what came over me, but my fears quickly dissipated as I began to speak. I don't know if it was divine intervention, my overly-prepared content, or simply letting go of everyone's opinion, but I had a job to do, and this product line had an opportunity to transform our business for the better.

Those same physiological reactions of anxiety (racing heart, increased rate of speech), actually transformed into a show of genuine excitement and positive energy, and the crowd was feeding off that energy. *How is this happening?* I wondered. I was in an out-of-body experience as applause and laughter responded to my attempts at humor. Despite letting go of other's opinions, I was actually receiving a very positive response.

When I left the stage, I high-fived my boss and noticed my hands were shaking—not from fear, but adrenaline. My colleague and I co-led the presentations that week, and were given praise on how well the launch went. We had set a new bar for the company, and our team was excited and ready to change the world with the launch.

I've done hundreds of presentations since that day, and I haven't experienced those nerves again. When you focus on a higher purpose, you stop worrying about what other people think. In the end, it's not about you. It never was.

I'm still amazed at the range of emotions I felt that day: worried about the moment, what other people were thinking, if I was up to the task, etc. Then, making a decision to bet on myself and say, "I've got this." And letting it rip.

As our esteem grows, we build the vulnerability to look at ourselves with honesty and empathy. We dare to step into the arena. Despite our failures, we can pick ourselves up and continue to fight. We inevitably learn to conquer our demons and build confidence by telling ourselves we can do hard things. As you step into the arena of life, your Authentic Voice will conquer the Mammoth. And then the fun can begin.

Abraham Maslow recognized the importance of a healthy evaluation of ourselves, self-respect, and the esteem of others. Thwarting these needs, according to Maslow, produced feelings of inferiority, weakness, and helplessness. For any aspiring leader who wants to make a positive change in the world around them, their esteem needs have to be anchored like an oak tree. Hone the skill of self-talk in challenging moments. Filter other people's feedback when everyone has an opinion about everything.

As Oscar Wilde said, "Be yourself. Everyone else is already taken."

Key Themes: Esteem

- ➲ Vulnerability isn't a weakness; it's the most accurate measurement of courage. Vulnerability is about accepting your imperfections and not being held back by them.
- ➲ High performers have a higher tolerance for discomfort and can thrive under pressure. They seek challenging circumstances to push their edges and see what they can do. They relish

a challenge, but don't stake their personal identity on their outcomes.

➲ Sport and Performance Psychologist Michael Gervais termed the phrase FOPO, Fear of Other People's Opinions, as one of the greatest constrictors of human potential.

➲ Gervais believes a personal philosophy central to your values and beliefs can overcome FOPO. When the strength of your values and beliefs are more significant than the fear of other's opinions, your full potential can be unleashed.

Maslow Magic: The Magic in the Application

➲ What areas of your career are you your harshest critic? How does that hold you back? Write out 3-5 examples where you have thrived under pressure, and came through when the stakes were high. These are your reference points to remind yourself you can do hard things.

➲ How have you let FOPO (Fear of Other People's Opinions) hold you back in the past? What did it cost you?

➲ What are your unshakeable values and beliefs that supersede other's opinions? Why is it important to disregard the chatter and rise up to the challenge? What's on the line if you can't rise against the haters? How can you be your own self-coach?

CHAPTER 6

COGNITIVE NEEDS
The Creative Spark

"We are going to recommend an MRI," said the physician. My wife and I were investigating a potential medical condition for one of my children, and struggling to find a solid answer. As parents, we often fear for the health of our children—especially when we're left sitting idly by without answers. Best to worst case scenarios were running through my mind. *What will happen if the test presents this way? Or that way?* We were sitting in the dark, completely dependant on the outcome of the test. *And about the test—how do we know if those results will be accurate?* So many what ifs.

Letting go of my child into the hands of the health care provider and MRI machine was excruciating. Many children are terrified of the MRI experience. They are forced to sit in a tight, claustrophobic space, with loud bangs and thumps during the scan. Children are often not fully aware of why they need an MRI test, or why they have to be so still for an extended period of time, an often impossible feat for a child. Worse yet, the child is left alone to confront their fears without the comfort of parents.

MRI scanners were first installed in the 1980's, and over forty years later, we haven't really improved the patient experience, especially for our most vulnerable populations. General Electric understood this problem when selling MRI machines for pediatric patients.[86] Customers were challenging them to improve patient experience and make the procedure less frightening for young children. Before an MRI takes place, 80 percent of children need to be sedated because of how terrifying the MRI machine is—a real problem, and one we now had to struggle with concerning our own child. The BOOM-BOOM-BOOM would turn into the tunnel of doom for a child.

Maslow on Creativity

With additional experience and study, Maslow recognized the more advanced end of the hierarchy left out essential sub-components of "peak experiences." In 1970, the same year he died, he published his final update to the timeless hierarchy in a book titled *Motivation and Personality.*

The first addition to his original theory focused on cognitive or creative needs. Maslow recognized that once basic esteem levels were met, individuals often had a greater need to learn and explore.

Some of these traits show up as creativity, foresight, curiosity, and meaning. High performers desire and are willing to dive into the unknown and figure things out. They want to learn more and create more—to learn for learning's sake.

Maslow challenged the idea that only certain individuals could be creative. "The key question isn't what fosters creativity? But it is why...isn't everyone creative? Where was the human potential lost? How was it crippled? I think therefore a good question might be not why do people create but why do people not create or innovate? We have got to abandon the sense of amazement in the face of creativity, as if it were a miracle if anybody created anything."[87]

Everyone has the potential to be creative. When we engage in creative activities, we tap into a deep well of inspiration and imagination to connect with our true selves and others. By exploring our creative potential, we discover new talents, passions, and interests, enriching our lives and bringing us a sense of fulfillment and joy.

Creative needs also promote innovation and progress, encouraging us to think outside the box and develop new solutions to problems. Ultimately, by fulfilling our creative needs, we can unlock our full potential and contribute to the betterment of society as a whole.

Leaders are Readers

President Harry S. Truman once said, "Not all readers are leaders, but all leaders are readers." Reading and the overall accumulation of knowledge is a common trait for highly successful performers.

John Coleman from the Harvard Business Review wrote an article describing the leadership benefits of reading:[88]

> Evidence suggests that reading can improve intelligence and lead to innovation and insight. Some studies have shown, for example, that reading makes you smarter through a larger vocabulary and more world knowledge in addition to abstract reasoning skills. Reading—whether Wikipedia, Michael Lewis, or Aristotle—is one of the quickest ways to acquire and assimilate new information. Many business people claim that reading across fields is good for creativity. And leaders who can

sample insights in other fields, such as sociology, the physical sciences, economics, or psychology, and apply them to their organizations are more likely to innovate and prosper.

Coleman gives five quick tips to create a more meaningful reading life.

➲ *Join a reading group:* Find a group of friends who will dive into the same writing and take time to understand everyone's perspective on what they read. It could differ from your own.

➲ *Vary your reading:* If you read the same subject, commit to reading a few books outside your comfort zone or in another genre.

➲ *Apply your reading to your work:* This is a no-brainer. If you are struggling with a business problem at work, dive into books that address your situation.

➲ *Encourage others:* Tim Ferriss is often intrigued by what books people gift most often, in order to understand what books have had meaning and what they find most valuable. It might do the same for others.

➲ *Read for fun:* Reading fiction can be a great opportunity to escape mentally, which is why beach reading is so popular. Reading creative stories at night might help you fall asleep faster than a data-intensive nonfiction book.

However you choose, applying a reading habit can have compounding benefits for your career. If you don't have a reading habit today, start with a genre you enjoy. I didn't particularly like reading as a child, and taking my teacher's advice, my mother introduced sports books to me, which drew my interest. This introduction was the starting point for an insatiable desire to learn and grow through books. Reading will soon become something you look forward to instead of something you dread.

Silicon Valley and Creativity

They've just got that creative gene. How often have you heard a similar comment to describe someone who has "it"? They are the most innovative in the room, skilled at conjuring up something new and brainstorming endless ideas. They are willing to jump far outside normal everyday thinking to establish a new concept.

Over the years, people have made mistaken assumptions about creativity through the lens of business.[89] Conventional wisdom stated that the "creatives" differed from the calculated "business people." The creatives were undisciplined, free spirits, while the business types were goal-driven, heavily analytical, hardworking people focused on rational logic. The two didn't have a coexistence.

However, some of the best in business have been significant innovators, like Walt Disney, Steve Jobs, Jeff Bezos, and Elon Musk. They have been able to balance creativity and focused execution.

Another myth about creativity and innovation is that everything starts from one big idea. While this can occasionally happen, most large-scale innovation comes from incremental innovation, tiny improvements layering over time.

The next false assumption is that innovators happen to get it right all of the time. But the opposite is true. Innovators may not be the most creative, but they have the most practice doing something new. Thomas Edison had many failures with the light bulb, and his constant attempts eventually led to one of the most significant breakthroughs for humanity.

Another common misconception about creativity and innovation is that the original idea is the hard part, and everything else falls into place. Developing an idea is fun, but then you need to explore and test it. Not everyone will agree with you, but you take the relevant feedback, disregard the rest, and iterate again.

And keep trying and testing until you get it right. Creativity takes work!

It's easy to fall into the above narratives, assuming you either have the creative gene or don't. Analytical types don't mesh with the creators who wear Hawaiian shirts to work and think outside the box.

The analytics are focused and deliberate, while the creatives are all over the place. So, to test some of the above assumptions, I planted myself in one of the global hubs of innovation, Silicon Valley. For the last 70 years, nestled in the southern part of San Francisco Bay, this area is known for its crossover of government, university, and private enterprise in pursuit of delivering what's next.

The area's innovative roots trace back to Bill Hewlett and David Packard and their development of the audio oscillator in the late 1930s. Their invention was born in their garage, inspiring generations of innovators to begin their ideation process in their garages.

As time progressed and the semiconductor and internet arrived, Silicon Valley has seen exponential growth, with major companies like Apple, Google, Cisco Systems, eBay, Meta Platforms (founder of Facebook), X (formerly Twitter), and Salesforce all taking root in the area. A disproportionate amount of meaningful innovation has occurred in Silicon Valley.

But what makes this area so fertile for innovation? While it certainly has one of the most innovation-friendly climates and attracts great talent, innovation doesn't just magically happen, right?

With additional research, I learned that Design Thinking was the foundational process for many innovators in the region. Design thinking is used for more than solving simple, run-of-the-mill problems in today's society. In the early 1970s, Theorist Horst Rittel's challenged designers to move beyond the simple and towards "wicked problems," defined as problems that are open, complex, and ambiguous.[90]

Some scholars trace the roots of design thinking back to John Dewey in 1935, with the melding of aesthetics and engineering principles.

However, the term has grown more mainstream with David Kelley's Silicon Valley innovation boutique, IDEO. David founded IDEO in 1978, and has been at the forefront of product and process improvement innovation for decades.[91]

Kelley has been behind many of Silicon Valley's leading innovations, including the first computer mouse, at the request of Steve Jobs and Apple. David later founded Stanford University's Hasso Plattner Institute of Design, commonly known as the "d.school." The d.school's mission is to inject "creative confidence" into the world, driving a philosophical framework for collaborative teamwork to tackle today's wicked problems.

After finding myself in creative projects and hearing about the school of design, I traveled to Silicon Valley in 2018 to learn how this process can help anyone become creative. In a one-week intensive program titled the Stanford d.school Design Thinking Bootcamp, I learned the principles of this process and its inspiration.

The Design Thinking framework employs five basic steps toward producing some of the most significant innovations in the world.[92] Simply put, the process can be broken down as follows:

- ➲ Empathy: Understanding the unique pain points of your end-user's experience.
- ➲ Define: Properly define the problem to solve based on your end-user.
- ➲ Ideation: Brainstorming for multiple solutions that may solve the problem.
- ➲ Prototype: Picking the best themes and putting together a basic, no-frills prototype to test your hypothesis against the problem.
- ➲ Test: Testing your prototype to see what is working and what is not.
- ➲ Refine: Continually improve and test your idea until you get it right.

This process works best with repetition. Innovation is often not just a great idea birthed into the world for massive change; instead, innovation is a unique understanding of your end-user and a focused process to iterate and test your solutions. As you'll see, innovation rarely comes from a Eureka! moment. Rather, it is a continual process of testing and refining until we get it right.

Empathy

The first law of Design Thinking is to remember you are not designing for yourself but for a different end-user. As much as we think we understand others' feelings, we don't understand their point of view until we walk in their shoes. While your idea or solution sound greats to you, there might be better options for the person or customer segment you are designing for. Your end-user could be an external customer who wants a particular product or service, or an internal customer who wants an improved process or creative solution.

Immediately connecting with the human experience is vital for innovation, not just looking at a set of facts and evidence. It's all about how the end-user is experiencing the world around them. We need to see life as they see it and walk through their shoes to understand their unique challenges.

I remember an exercise I did when branding a product for an upcoming launch. We hired a consultancy to guide us through the process, gaining a large set of opinions and perspectives on our various options.

I had one particular product name I was very fond of and thought it was the obvious choice. When our surveys went out and the feedback came in, the name I was so sure of was dead last on the list of 12 other options.

Not only did I have no clue what my customers were thinking, but I also didn't realize they really *disliked* my choice. I had to swallow my pride in order to understand what my audience was thinking, feeling, and experiencing.

When entering the Empathy stage, we must drop our assumptions, biases, and judgments, which can be hard but necessary if we create meaningful work. To be objective towards our customers' viewpoints, we can look at several data collections, both qualitative and quantitative, to get to the root of their experience. We want to understand their emotions because these feelings can trigger a particular challenge they may not be able to articulate verbally.

During the empathy stage of design thinking, we immerse ourselves in our customer's experience through research, interviews, surveys, shadowing, or customer journey mapping.[93] We can visually plot out our customers' experience and note any breaks in the process which might cause friction for our customers. There are many ways to understand our customer's point of view. Whatever way we choose to understand our customer's point of view, we need to discard our persona and take on our customers.

Customers may have explicit pain points which are fairly obvious. But implicit pain points are less clear, occurring when a customer's frustration inhibits them from getting to the root of their problem and they need help articulating it. Figuring out this need for the customer is the magic in the design process.

As the facts roll in, we must stay objective and not tie ourselves to any outcome, keeping in mind that it's not just about what the end-user is saying but also what they are experiencing.

Define

After extensively researching our topic, we start to unpack the data and the facts. To simplify the topic, we need to synthesize details and group significant data points into major themes by asking questions.

What did the end-user articulate as a significant concern? Are there gaps in our research? Bottlenecks in the customer experience? Are there communication challenges when hitting a roadblock? Since different personas will look at other ways of experiencing the problem, try to understand what and why they are doing it.

Feelings and emotions signal if you are onto something. And more input from your teammates can draw connections between data points. Visuals, whiteboards, and Post-it notes can pull out the raw hypotheses from the group.

One common technique some designers use here is the "Curious Child" exercise. We love children's curiosity, as the entire world is a blank slate open to exploration. We also know that children can ask A LOT of questions; sometimes they are looking for a satisfactory answer, while others are just looking to see how far you will go. Diving into this nuance can be completely maddening, yet extremely interesting at other times.

So, let's put it to use. Let's say two friends are out to dinner at a cash-only restaurant. When the check comes, both friends grab their wallets or purses to reach for money. Except one friend stops in horror.

But why? Shocked, they realize they forgot to bring cash to pay for their meal.

But why? They were running late for a few meetings today and couldn't find a good ATM en route to the restaurant.

But why? The ATMs in the area aren't affiliated with banks and look sketchy in the local convenience stores. They charge exorbitant fees and look ripe for a fraudster to steal your ATM pin information.

Here is a major point of frustration.

But why? The friend without cash has plenty of money and a successful career, which makes them even more frustrated.

But why? They are embarrassed because they must admit to their friend they don't have any money. What will their friend think? That they are irresponsible or a freeloader? These thoughts increase their anxiety.

But why? The friend will feel guilty when the other friend picks up the check on their own, obsessing about it all afternoon and going out of their way to find a safe ATM to grab some money. They will think about it while driving out of their way to find their friend to repay the money. The extra driving may cause them to miss their kid's soccer game at night.

But why? Because the cashless friend wants to be seen as reliable. They want to be free from guilt and know their friendship remains intact.

So, what are we solving for? Embarrassment. Harder access to cash. Taking time away from other planned activities to find a reliable ATM. But how do you make this a clear problem statement?

Clarifying your problem first is essential to the rest of the design thinking process. In this scenario, the problem statement could be, "How might we provide better access to cash without an ATM nearby?"

Or we could make it a personal point of view statement. (Someone) needs a way to (action) because (insight). In this case, Peter needs a way to give Mary cash because he is embarrassed about not paying his bill.

Sound familiar? This scenario is similar to the birth of Venmo when the founder struggled to pay a restaurant bill with a friend.[94] There was a clear need for more frictionless access to cash wherever you were.

Your mind may naturally offer solutions quickly, but patiently and thoroughly defining the problem will yield important insight. By defining a good problem statement, dare to take a big leap to a real game-changing insight. This insight will be the launching pad for an incredible ideation session!

Ideation (Divergent Thinking)

With our problem clearly defined, we can enter into one of the most exciting aspects of Design Thinking, the ideation phase.[95] In this phase, we want to generate many ideas, without fixating on their quality. This phase can be especially fun with a group of people, generating as much creative energy as possible. We can use whiteboards, Post-it notes, mind maps, etc. In the ideation stage, the only rule is suspending judgment.

Pointing out the flaws in others' ideas as impractical or far-fetched is easy, but these critiques will limit the creative output from the group. Don't worry about the concept being pragmatic enough. Innovation stems from uniqueness, not always relevance. During this phase, we are looking for divergent thinking. How broad and wide can we push the ideas to be unique?

In your group, you will have all sorts of creative styles. Some will be very expressive and very verbal while others will want to visualize their idea through a sketch. But everything is relevant. While extroverts might easily contribute, introverts might be afraid and unsure when to speak. However, introverts can frequently be some of the deepest-thinking, most thoughtful people on the planet. Make sure everyone has a voice to throw an idea on the table.

A helpful exercise in this phase is the "Yes, and..." exercise, which is a popular approach improv comics use to get the creative juices flowing in the warm-up process. Let's say we have seven people in our group and want to build out seven ideas.

We start with one team member speaking an original idea out loud. The following person will say, "Yes, and..." to add another detail to the story. The following person will say "Yes, and..." with another piece. And so on, and so on.

This exercise can be entertaining while building on novelty and crowd wisdom. Allowing everyone to participate and layer onto an idea can add several options pulling the group together. Not to mention, it can also be a lot of fun!

Another ideation tactic can be to look at how different industries solve similar problems. For example, what can an appliance manufacturing company learn about service delivery from a pizza company? What can vaccine clinics learn from a fast-food drive-thru? This tactic played out when a backlogged COVID-19 vaccine clinic sourced ideas from the local Chick-fil-A drive-thru.[96]

The ideation phase can be one of the most enjoyable parts of the creative process in design thinking. By suspending judgment, asking everyone to participate, and pushing for quantity over quality, you can generate so many useful ideas for later in the process.

Innovative ideas stem from uniqueness and not just relevance. Consider this an opportunity to suspend our overly pragmatic brain to search for what's truly possible.

Prototype (Convergent Thinking)

I'm often amazed at my children's creative freedom, particularly with the unused Amazon boxes sent to my house. When my children were young, a new box would equal a new toy. My children quickly grabbed the box, a set of markers, duct tape, and any other inexpensive arts and crafts to begin to create just about anything. Depending on the box size, I have seen pirate ships, forts, pet frog homes, Halloween masks, you name it. No idea was too far-fetched to prototype a design. This boundless creativity serves as a segue into our next phase of design thinking, the prototype stage.

The goal of the prototype stage is to take some of the raw ideas from the ideation phase and bring them to life. In this convergent stage, we want to narrow down the basic brainstorming from the ideation phase.

Consistent with other Design Thinking stages, perfection is the enemy of progress. We want to start building something that represents our ideas, but not get too wrapped up in labor-intensive or time-consuming details. Speed is important! Building faster prototypes can lead to quicker feedback sessions and more improvement.

You can use mock-ups with paper prototypes, basic office supplies, and even wireframes for a physical product.[97] You can use walk-throughs or role-plays with real people to capture the whole experience. You can use storyboards to turn words into pictures of how the new design would work.

We want to bring our ideas to life, to leap off the page, so we can begin the conversation. Prototypes allow us to test the design features with minimal resources, a much faster process to accelerate learning. They also quickly iterate our product design to correct aspects of the structure after receiving end-user feedback.

Don't try to be perfect; embracing failure is okay. The top worldwide designers do not welcome negative feedback as proof they need to be more competent to design great ideas. Instead, they use feedback as an opportunity to get better. A rough prototype allows you to quickly assemble your product concept without a lengthy production process, getting to the truth of the product while being less expensive than waiting for perfection.

Our end goal of the prototype stage is to get to what is commonly referred to as a "Minimal Viable Product" or MVP for short, a term coined by author Eric Ries.[98] A minimal viable product is a version of the product with minimal features to attract one customer. Once we have one customer, we look for ways to improve the design to attract five customers. From five customers to 50. From 50 to 500. From 500 to 5 million. In his book The Startup Way, Ries outlined an interesting project he did with General Electric (GE).

GE was known for a massive production process for industrial equipment, which often took years and millions of sunk costs before a product even shipped. By incorporating a fast MVP approach, GE could handle a project that normally took five years and shipped it in 6 months.[99]

By getting feedback early with a small set of customers, you can make the appropriate tweaks to move quickly with more impact than waiting for a perfect design. But first, you have to embrace the necessary imperfections to get feedback in the first place. Suspend judgment on your idea (and yourself) when getting your first designs out.

Test

We can properly test our ideas with a potential subset of end-users with a prototype.[100] These users could be customers, other employees who will be the recipient of your ideas, or anyone who will fully experience your design.

A famous quote from General George Patton regarding quick decisions has always intrigued me: "A good plan violently executed today is better than a perfect plan next week."[101] In war, where the stakes are highest, Patton recognized that paralysis by analysis can sometimes mean the difference between life and death. While the stakes for our idea may have fewer consequences than war, consider some interesting parallels.

When testing your concept, we must ensure we get the right "type" of end-users in the room. Only some end-users will embrace new ideas. Everett Rogers from Iowa State coined this process with his popular Adoption Curve (also called the Diffusion process) in 1962.[102]

Some early risk-taking innovators strongly desire to be the "first" to use anything. These people line up at the Apple store for the new iPhone release, a product they have yet to learn about. But they want to be the first.

Next is a group of "Early Adopters." This group is also very progressive and comfortable taking social risks, but pursues new ideas with less enthusiasm than an early innovator. Their feedback is still essential and you can learn much from them.

You have the early majority, late majority, and laggards following the early adopters. These groups may not be your best test subjects early on, as they need more information and experience before making decisions.

Early innovators and adopters tend to be more forgiving of mistakes, seeing an opportunity for improvement versus just writing off the idea as a total fail. Since they love to be a part of the early process, they can be valuable in the design stage.

You don't need a huge group of end-users to test your prototype, but you do need substantial enough feedback to gain a few general ideas on how to iterate and improve. Every product has a life cycle and adoption process for its end-users.

Proper testing with potential end-users is invaluable to your creative process. In writing this book, I approached 15 potential readers in the leadership genre to ask for feedback after completing the first manuscript. Their feedback was pure gold, with similar themes on what was good and what could be improved. I took their feedback to heart, made the adjustments, and had a much better product prior to going through a full edit. In any creative pursuit, the ability to test and refine will significantly improve your final product.

Refine and Iterate

Some projects do have an end date. A movie has been released. A book is published. Brochures are printed. Internal processes are finally implemented. Our ideas are sent out for the world to see.

However, we can often be stuck in an infinite loop of refining and iterating our solution. Think about all the app updates for your computer or smartphone. These products are in an endless improvement process to upgrade the end-user's experience.

You will receive helpful feedback as you test your concepts in the world. You may find it necessary to return to other parts of the design journey to implement better improvements, truly getting to the heart of the problem.

You may need to return to the empathy stage to ensure you are solving the right problem. Is your problem accurately defined? Or you may need to go back to the ideation phase and think of more possible solutions that have tangible value.

Or you have the right ideas but may have picked the wrong concept to prototype and create. Or the last prototype needs adjusting in a few minimal ways.

Whatever it may be, as innovators, we are in an endless loop of iteration to continually improve our end-users' experience in the world. This loop starkly contrasts the idea that creatives live in this bubble where one good idea strikes, and the rest is history. True innovation requires a process and science!

If your solutions are taking forever, you're in good company. Thomas Edison famously took 1,000 attempts at the light bulb. WD-40 is aptly named as the company underwent 40 iterations until finally creating the rust-prevention product. WD-40 stands for "Water displacement perfected on the 40th try."[103]

When you first learn the design thinking process, you may want to share everything you learned with everyone and how it will change the world! However, convincing some coworkers will take time.

When gaining buy-in from your company, please don't feel obligated to describe the entire Design Thinking process, gaining a fanatical following overnight. It may be too overwhelming for some people, especially if they subscribe to the idea that creative people do all their innovation in lightbulb moments.

Jeremy Utley, leader of the Stanford d. School's Design thinking bootcamp, suggests that we focus on show over tell.[104] Demonstrate the process in principles one step at a time. If you need new insights, bring in an end-user. To test a concept, make a rough prototype to visualize your idea. Repeating these steps will prove that Design Thinking is worth imbedding in your organization's DNA.

At Peace on a Pirate Ship

Stuck in the challenge of pediatric experience, General Electric went through the Design Thinking process for the MRI experience with children. Through the Empathy and Define stages, GE learned how MRIs horrified many of these pediatric patients. The MRI test was necessary for their condition, but how could they improve the user experience? Through the collective design team's imagination during the ideation stage, GE decided to revamp the MRI machine into a real-life pirate adventure.

Here's how it works: the operator tells the child they will be sailing inside the pirate ship and must stay completely still while on the boat. After their trip, they pick a small gift from the "pirate's treasure chest." Decals depicting a pirate adventure decorate the whole room.

GE also used an MRI machine to create a space adventure, and the pediatric patients were told the BOOM-BOOM-BOOM stage occurred when the spaceship went into hyperdrive. Through GE's creative approach to solving a problem, children began *looking forward* to going on the MRI "ride." One even asked if they could return the next day to do it again. Patient satisfaction scores rose 90 percent without any changes to the underlying technology.

When my son's MRI tests came back completely normal, my wife and I breathed a sigh of relief. Our worst fears would not be coming to fruition. Though my son didn't get a chance to ride on the pirate ship or space adventure, I'm comforted to know that future pediatric patients have the potential for a significantly different experience.

Abraham Maslow's view of creativity wasn't focused on the few creatives who inspire the world with new ideas, as if it were a lottery system. On the contrary, Maslow focused on how *everyone* can be creative. The process of innovation is an exciting one with multiple twists and turns. You never know what alley you may head down as you ideate and test your ideas. In a competitive global marketplace, innovation is not only for a select few but necessary for everyone. Maslow was right. We shouldn't be surprised when we discover creativity. The truth is everyone can be creative!

Key Themes: Cognitive

- ➲ Leaders are readers. Strong reading habits can help you source ideas from history's most brilliant minds.
- ➲ The design thinking process has been a staple for creativity within Silicon Valley and many other innovative projects.
- ➲ Anyone can be a "creative." Following the design thinking process (Empathy, Define, Ideation, Prototype, Test, Refine) is a proven system to drive new ideas for new products and processes.
- ➲ When implementing design thinking in your organization, focus on show over tell. Break off a few components and introduce them individually, instead of overloading your team with a new "system." Over time, the pieces will coincide as new creative DNA in your organization.

Maslow Magic: The Magic in the Application

➲ What part of your business needs a creative overhaul? What's at risk if you can't change? Write out a paragraph on the negative effects of not launching a much-needed creative project?

➲ Identify one opportunity to run through the design thinking process over the next 30 days. Who should be involved? Why are their voices important for the project? What can you gain from walking in the end-user's shoes, properly defining the problem, using ideation, building the prototype, and testing and refining?

CHAPTER 7

AESTHETIC NEEDS

Beauty is in the Eye of the Beholder

It was 5:01 pm and just like clockwork, the call I was expecting came through. I was a sales representative in the medical technology sector, and our company's product leaders had just informed us a key product line had an issue with a supplier, leading to a major backorder predicted to last months. Since this was an essential portfolio product, I knew it would be a rough road ahead. As a sales person, my mind instantly questioned how I would reach my sales quota without this key product line. Or deal with the angry customers when I couldn't deliver. Or the competitors who were waiting to pounce on the opportunity to fill in our gaps.

One of my fellow sales colleagues—the one on the other end of the line—loved to complain about our company's shortcomings. He was known to fly off the handle emotionally when things didn't go the way he had planned, and phone calls with him tended to be negative and soul-draining. He loved to harp on his perspective about the company's poor decisions, his perception of our leadership, and how the grass was greener at other companies.

"Here we go again!" he said. "First, they raise our sales quotas, and now they won't even give us the products to hit that unachievable quota. This place SUCKS!!"

I tried to be calm and pragmatic, explaining that this was certainly not welcome news but we would find a way to move forward. After all, we had been through this before. I know I had to work to make sure my customers could find another option. I also knew this might free up time for me to focus on the under-focused product lines needing my attention.

My colleague wasn't finished, though. He had more to get off his chest. "What type of buffoons are running this place? Do they even understand what we're going through every day? We're late for product launches, can't deliver on the products we do have, and they decide to spring this on us last minute. I have a new product trial with a hospital next week, and now I need to tell them we can't do it."

As he went on and on, the minutes felt like days. I tried to let him vent, get whatever it was off his chest, and then look for a path forward. Our company had weathered storms in the past, and we can weather this one as well. Still, these phone calls were beginning to crush me. I later learned I wasn't the only one to whom he vented. In fact, he would vent to everyone. It was like he was a politician trying to lobby support for his negative perceptions. If it wasn't about a backorder, it would be something else: office gossip or some other complaint.

I started hoping I would hit a bad pocket of cell service on my drive home so the call would break up. Every time I saw his number on my caller ID, I felt a heavy weight on my chest, and this day was no different.

Here we go again.

Maslow on Aesthetics

As previously discussed, Maslow recognized his basic set of needs, published in 1943, was incomplete. Maslow felt a deeper need for appreciation of beauty in the complete life.

In Maslow's third edition of *Motivation and Personality*, he recognized a need for aesthetics but realized we understand less about this need than others. He identified that at least some people have a fundamental aesthetic need.

"They get sick (in special ways) from ugliness and are cured by beautiful surroundings; they crave actively, and their cravings can be satisfied only by beauty. It is seen almost universally in healthy children. Some evidence of such an impulse is found in every culture and in every age as far back as the cave dwellers."

Aesthetic needs include order, symmetry, closure, system, and structure, all pointing to a basic need for beauty, balance, and design.

Aesthetic needs can be a lens through which to see the world. But if you drop your sunglasses into a pile of mud, it's easy to focus on the muck in the world. How can we escape it? We live in a 24-hour news cycle sensationalizing violence and stoking fear and division in our society. Social media forces us to compete with others' imaginary lives in their manufactured highlight reels. Considering all this negativity, seeing the world through a disparaging and self-defeating lens is easy.

However, mastery of aesthetics can be a primer for higher engagement in your life and craft. This section will explore the launching pad of our higher-level needs, undoubtedly putting you in a better position to experience the world. The four horsemen of the aesthetics needs are grace, gratitude, optimism, and mindfulness. We will explore the role of each to create our optimal lens of fulfillment.

Grace

The role of grace can be powerful if we stop to recognize it, and can appear in many terms. Some call it God. Some call it the universe. Some call it Karma. Others refer to it as luck.

Whatever you may call it, high achievers recognize that the forces of good in the world are more powerful than evil. The paranoid have difficulty understanding this dynamic because it's difficult to prove but that doesn't mean it doesn't exist. It also doesn't mean we always get what we want or that we will always be victorious. But it's there. If our intent is pure and our will is strong, we recognize grace can sometimes push us through. The more we acknowledge grace, the more it seems to appear.

Tony Robbins beautifully described the gift of grace.[105] "The gift of grace is a chance to start fresh. It's a chance to be free, a chance to let love flow to yourself at a new level. Understanding grace is the key to being able to let go. Let go of what others have done to you, and let go of what you may have done to others, even unintentionally. It is a peace and tranquility that can only come from knowing that life happens for you, not to you."

Imagine that. Life is happening for us, not to us. While it's easy to see the gift of grace when things go well, can we recognize how perceived negative events push us to a better place at times? A romantic relationship ends poorly but directs you to your lifetime partner. You don't get the job you wanted, but later find out the company you interviewed went out of business a year later. You get a failing grade on a test, but it drives a passion to build better study habits you maintain for the rest of your life.

Can you look at every event in your life as something happening for you, not against you? The Latin phrase *Amor Fati* is a concept many ancient philosophers have embraced. This concept has been attributed to Roman Emperor Marcus Aurelius, Greek slave turned philosopher

Epictetus, and German Philosopher Fredrich Nietzsche. Regardless of the source, this phrase means accepting and relishing your fate.

Author Ryan Holiday describes this concept well. "Yes, it's a little unnatural to love things we never wanted to happen in the first place. But what other, worse adversities might this one be saving us from? What might we learn from this unchosen experience? What good, equally unexpected events might result from it? We know that in retrospect, we often look back at difficult times fondly, almost wistfully, so we might as well feel that now."[106]

Former Navy Seal and now author and speaker Jocko Willink has a process he calls "Good" when life hands him lemons[107]:

- ⊃ Oh, the mission got canceled? Good...We can focus on another one.
- ⊃ Didn't get the new high-speed gear we wanted? Good...We can keep it simple.
- ⊃ Didn't get promoted? Good...More time to get better.
- ⊃ Didn't get funded? Good...We own more of the company.
- ⊃ Didn't get the job you wanted? Good...Go out, gain more experience, and build a better resume.
- ⊃ Got injured? Good...Needed a break from training.
- ⊃ Got tapped out? Good...It's better to tap out in training than tap out on the street.
- ⊃ Got beat? Good...We learned.
- ⊃ Unexpected problems? Good...We have to figure out a solution.

Taking this approach doesn't mean you are avoiding reality or blind to the things that need addressed. You recognize every setback as an opportunity to improve and get better.

Your failures are not a personal indictment of who you are as a human or your talents; it's just feedback and an opportunity for improvement.

As a recovering perfectionist, I know this gift too well. Even if it was one of the most difficult virtues to learn, it offered the most freedom when conquered. Early in my career, I would beat myself up for every minor failure, holding back a key learning opportunity when challenges arose. I would eventually come to terms with the lessons, but I made myself miserable in the process for anything short of perfection. Not a fun way to go about your day, which is why grace is so essential.

Equally essential is showing grace to others. If we agree that good overwhelms evil, recognizing those same forces at work in others is important. It's easy to be kind to ourselves yet criticize others for their most minor mistakes. But the same universal laws apply to everyone. Assuming the best intent in others is a doorway to peace. Most people don't want to do the wrong thing, so let them off the hook if they make a mistake. See it is a chance to teach and learn, not a chance to condemn. They got it wrong, but they were trying.

We all make mistakes, and nobody lives a perfect life. Give the same level of grace to others as you would yourself. As mentioned earlier, we estimate that up to four percent of the population could be sociopaths, which is a relatively small number compared to the greater population. 96 percent of people, at their heart, are trying to do the right thing.

I would be equally as harsh with others as I was to my own failures. While I was never one to have a high level of conflict, I would internalize others' failures like a judge in a courtroom. As I matured over time, I realized that most people aren't trying to harm others or be difficult, and they actually have the best of intentions. Taking a moment to look at the world through their eyes, their decisions make sense, even if misguided. And on some occasions, they may be correct in their actions.

So, chances are, we will be working and involved with people with good intentions for themselves and their loved ones during the day.

And on occasion, they may fall.

Recognize that they are doing their best just like you. Giving grace is a chance for healing, connection, and trust.

Gratitude

With grace as a foundation, gratitude is another step to seeing beauty in yourself and all around you. The great Roman orator Cicero wrote, "Gratitude is not only the greatest of virtues but the parent of all the others."[108]

Gratitude is when a person attributes at least a portion of the benefit they have received to something external (another person, event, spiritual force, etc.). We associate feelings of gratitude less frequently with negative emotions and more frequently with positive emotions, such as feeling energized, alert, and enthusiastic. Grateful people have been shown to have higher levels of positive affect, a greater sense of belonging, and lower levels of depression and stress.[109]

And gratitude is a trainable skill.

Incorporating a daily gratitude routine creates more repetition to "acknowledge" the good things happening in your life. Just like in weightlifting, more gratitude reps mean a stronger gratitude muscle.

Spiritual people often incorporate gratitude as a daily prayer to recognize the good things in their lives. Gratitude journals have also become a popular method to write down your daily wins, no matter how small.

With gratitude, you gain the positive effect of the event, and then double the benefit by acknowledging this event at a separate time of day. Lastly, knowing you will undertake this task later in the day, you will start looking for good things to write down. Surprisingly, you will discover many more good things are working than you previously thought. As this practice becomes a habit, gratitude strengthens and becomes a stronger presence in your life.

Optimism

As grace builds the foundation of a good and just world, gratitude is the appreciation of everything going well in life. These practices lead us to another key indicator of high performers: optimism.

Michael Gervais describes optimism as the belief that "something good is about to happen." He has never met a world-class performer who was a pessimist.[110]

One of the leading founders of positive psychology has been Martin Seligman, an author and psychologist from the University of Pennsylvania. Seligman is known for some of his early research on depression, and pioneered the famous study on learned helplessness in dogs.

He has written several books, including the bestseller *Learned Optimism*.[111] In an attempt to find the opposite of negativity, Seligman has been a pioneer in the field of positive psychology. Instead of focusing on what can go wrong, this psychology builds its origins around what can go right.

Seligman has found that the benefits of optimism are similar to gratitude. Optimistic people tend to have a better immune system and overall better health, making time to exercise more in their life. His works note how optimism helps cancer patients improve their immune systems.

In addition, Seligman noted that optimists performed better at their work. The insurance giant MetLife tried to understand why they had up to an 80 percent turnover rate at year four for members of their sales force. Seligman noted that a cohort of a slightly less-talented but highly optimistic group outperformed more talented but pessimistic employees. Drawing a similar conclusion, a study on children with math problems revealed that cynical students gave up earlier than those who remained optimistic.

Per Seligman, what sets optimists and pessimists apart is their "explanatory style." The explanatory style is how we talk to ourselves when things don't necessarily go our way.

The work of Albert Ellis, another early pioneer in American psychology, influenced Seligman. Ellis described the ABC technique.[112] which correlates to Adversity, Belief, and Consequence. Let's dive into one example with a pessimistic and optimistic style.

Let's say a love interest doesn't return our phone calls. Here's how a pessimist would decipher it:

> **Adversity:** My love interest isn't returning my calls.
> **Belief:** I am ugly or not funny.
> **Consequence:** I am an unlovable person.

That explanation is not very inspiring or encouraging.
Now, let's jump into how an optimistic style may handle it.

> **Adversity:** My love interest isn't returning my calls.
> **Belief:** Perhaps they didn't feel connected during our last date and lack the skill to have a more mature discussion to end the relationship gracefully.
> **Consequence:** I am worthy of so much more, and this situation redirects me to finding a better match.

Do you recognize the pattern? The pessimists tend to make their judgments universal, personal, and internal, while optimists tend to make event-specific judgments versus jumping to self-deprecation. They see adversity as a temporary occurrence, and they don't take it personally. Instead, they use it as a data point to recalibrate and improve the next time.

So, we often can't control what happens in the outside world, but we can change our beliefs towards what happens to establish a more productive consequence or action. The Grammy award-winning singer Jewel has a thoughtful exercise to explaining the events that occur in her life.[113]

When faced with adversity or setbacks, Jewel would take a piece of paper and write down three columns. The fear or belief she held went in the first column. The next column would be titled, "Why it's a lie."

The third column would reframe to provide a more productive explanation and next step. Her exercise showcases how we hold the power to give meaning to whatever happens in life. Because, remember, life is happening for you, not to you.

Like the gratitude journal, one option to reinforce optimism in your life is to consider everything going well in your day consistently. As the examples build over time, you condition your mind to see the good in the world and the endless possibilities. You have an archive of instances showcasing "good things happen to me."

Optimism is not built on blind faith, but a belief that things will work out if I am committed. Optimism is a trainable, necessary quality in a top performer but even more important in a leader.

Given the high-stakes world of the global marketplace, leaders with lower levels of optimism will be challenged to lead their teams authentically. Former U.S. General and Secretary of State Colin Powell once stated, "Perpetual optimism is a force multiplier."[114]

Mindfulness

Grace, gratitude, and optimism provide a magnificent lens to see the beauty and structure in the world around us, priming the brain to see all the possibilities. These three qualities condition us towards the practice of mindfulness, which helps us better recognize the present moment.

Mindfulness is the basic art of being present and aware of what's happening within and around us without judgment. It can be both a noun and a verb. Practicing mindfulness as a verb deliberately focuses on the present moment, the here and now. The noun state of being mindful is not being consumed with the past or concerned about the future. It's just where you are.

The scientific evidence detailing the complexity of mindfulness and its effect on humans is too expansive for the scope of this book. But we'll attempt to describe its surface benefits, hoping you will explore mindfulness more and how it fits into your life beyond this book.

Mindfulness is not a new concept but rather goes back over 2,000 years to the life of the original Buddha. And although it has roots in older traditions like Buddhism, Taoism, Stoicism, and Hinduism, it can also be found in other traditions like Christianity and Judaism. What once seemed isolated to monks and yogis has now entered mainstream practice with sports teams, schools, military organizations, etc. But how? And why?

My introduction to mindfulness was learning about Phil Jackson, the historic coach for the Chicago Bulls, during their magnificent championship run in the 1990s.[115] The public was in awe of Jackson, as he had successfully assembled a team of superstars who could play seamlessly together. He even convinced Michael Jordan, the game's greatest star, to have a more team-first mentality. His belief in Eastern practices, including meditation, informed his coaching style, and he took an interesting route to get there.

I picked up Jackson's book *Sacred Hoops* to learn more about his coaching style and what drove him. He described his playing style as anxiety-filled, and at times, angry. These feelings hindered his performance, but by recognizing the benefits of Eastern practice, including meditation, Jackson began to feel a greater sense of well-being and ability. The resulting feelings of calm and focus allowed him to center himself and perform at his best. As a coach, Jackson was determined to bring these same practices to his teams.

Published articles on mindfulness have significantly increased. In 1980, only a few articles were written on the topic. In 2008, 90 or so were published. Now, close to 1,000 articles per year are published on the subject of mindfulness.[116] Clearly, something in today's climate is driving this search for mindfulness and its daily application.

Modern-day life is inundated with distractions for our attention. A breaking news story appears on your phone. The buzz notification of a new email. Political division. Global health pandemics. The sense of urgency that everything needs to be done right now. The comparisons with the fake lives of others on social media and worrying about what others are thinking or saying about you.

Fear and anxiety are at an all-time high in modern-day culture. It's been estimated that 33.7 percent of people have some form of anxiety disorder in their lifetime.[117]

Adding to this research, a Harvard study showed that people think about something other than what they do 46.9 percent of the time.[118] Imagine that roughly half of the people you engaged with are somewhere else mentally. How frustrating to try and connect! And although mind wandering can sometimes be a springboard for creativity, prolonged stretches of time with a wandering mind can actually make us less happy. A greater sense of happiness and peace can come when living in the present moment.

Technology has permeated every facet of our lives, and smartphones have become a built-in distraction device. Steve Jobs, the iconic founder of Apple, famously introduced his "1984" ad during the 1984 Super Bowl, widely regarded as one of the greatest commercials of all time. The ad depicted a world controlled by a vague authority forcing everyone to fit in. Apple was poking fun at the Personal Computer culture at the time who played the role of Big Brother. By contrast, Apple's early days depicted their users as an eclectic counter-culture bunch, unafraid to be unique. Note the irony.

However, we have to explore how this technology has evolved. Apple's iPhones have become such a ubiquitous part of our everyday society we can hardly remember life without them.

With the constant notifications, buzzing, and distractions calling for attention, this device has a hold of our lives. Is Apple the new Big Brother? What Apple fought against in the 1980s is what they have become in modern times.

Now, more than ever, we need separation from the distraction to pay attention to what's inside.

Jon Kabat-Zinn is one of the trailblazers in the expansion of mindfulness in Western cultures, by founding the Mindfulness-Based Stress Reduction Clinic at the University of Massachusetts Medical School and the Center for Mindfulness in Medicine, Health Care, and Society. He authored many books and guided meditation programs, spreading mindfulness's practical application in modern cultures.[119]

His book *Wherever You Go, There You Are* is a bestselling classic. Many of the following principles come from Kabat-Zinn's work, and we are grateful for his contributions to the field.[120]

Mindfulness can counter the world's external stresses with immense benefits. Quite often, our minds are preoccupied with planning, thinking, and worrying about the future or obsessing over the past. Ignoring the present robs us of pouring our total creative energy into whatever we're doing. After all, our brain is wired to be alert for real or imagined danger, acting like monkeys, jumping from thought to thought, ruminating from worry to worry. This monkey mind prevents us from being in the moment and allows us to immerse ourselves in the here and now fully.

The only time we have is the present moment. We can't change the past or skip the scary future event we're anxious about. The only time we have is now. And if the next moment depends on this moment, doesn't it make sense to get it right, right now? Mindfulness allows us to free the mind by living in the present.

Over time, mindfulness can help us become calm and present in our relationships, allowing us to accept our authentic selves. You will create space to respond to events instead of a knee-jerk reaction in the moment. Viktor Frankl, a holocaust survivor and author of *Man's Search for Meaning,* has an enlightening take on this.[121] "Between stimulus and response there is a space. In that space is our power to choose our response. In our response lies our growth and our freedom." This response becomes easier to train with mindfulness.

Deep focus and calm create greater creativity and immersion in our activity, giving us a more fulfilling experience. Mindfulness is not a means to an end: the achievement of a flow state, the experience of peak moments in creative activity. However, the calm and deep focus stemming from mindfulness may allow us access to a flow state. In a world fighting for our attention, deep focus is a superpower.

You may tell yourself, wow, calm, deep focus, greater authenticity, deeper connections in relationships. Sign me up! If this sounds so good, what's the catch? The catch is that disciplined mindfulness requires you to move from doing to non-doing. Mindfulness will allow us to appreciate the beauty of the present moment, but to an achiever's mindset, it will seem counterintuitive. It doesn't feel like I am actually "doing" anything! Modern-day achievers may try to "achieve" mindfulness. But that's only possible once we accept the current reality of where we are today. After all, the only time we have is now.

If Maslow's hierarchy reveals a need to appreciate the world's beauty, we must start seeing the world for what it is using mindfulness as our pathway. Mindfulness can provide more present, intimate discussions with people we love, allow for a deep, focused flow state with our best creative work, and help us properly process (instead of suppress) challenging emotions and regulate.

In Tim Ferriss' book, *Tribe of Mentors*, he interviewed 140 people at the top of their fields. One of the most common similarities was a cultivated mindfulness or meditation practice.[122] So, doesn't finding a way to tap into this power more often make sense? After all, as Michael Gervais stated, "High performance lives in the present moment, where wisdom is revealed."[123]

So, how do you start a mindfulness practice? Begin with experimentation, since mindfulness takes many forms. Meditation is a common way to incorporate mindfulness in your life, as they are very similar practices. Mindfulness is the state of awareness of the present moment, and meditation is an activity to cultivate mindfulness and a stronger connection between the body and mind.

Several meditations exist to build these connections which are easy to incorporate in daily life when walking, sitting, lying, or eating. Try reciting a mantra or playing some light music in the background. Experiment with anything that gets your mind in a state of being fully present. As you'll discover, meditation is easier said than done, requiring discipline to cultivate.

As you begin to incorporate a mindfulness practice, just a few disclaimers. First, start small and have low expectations! I know low expectations are difficult for high achievers who want quick results, but I have never met a perfect meditator. When you begin meditation, you will recognize how quickly and easily your mind jumps from thought to thought.

Start with just one minute daily, progressing to five. Research shows that as few as thirteen minutes a day can decrease negative moods, enhance attention, increase working and recognition memory, and reduce anxiety scores.[124]

In order to begin, I will outline one of the more common (and simple) forms of meditation, using single-point breathing techniques. This meditation focuses on our breath going in and out, helping us form the connection between mind and body.

First, find a quiet room and time of the day to practice meditation. You want this time and space to be sacred. Start seated with your legs crossed and chest opened up. Some people prefer to try lying down, but the important thing is to be comfortable.

Inhale for 4 seconds, starting deep from your belly button and rising to your chest.

Hold your breath at the top for four seconds, focusing on the oxygen in your lungs and your general body state. Then, slowly, begin to exhale over an eight count.

Gradually release the air and notice how your body feels.

This practice may seem counterintuitive, with being present and paying attention to your body your only goal. At first, you will notice how quickly your mind wants to jump to something "productive." You will start thinking about your afternoon meeting, what you should pack the kids for lunch, or that jerk who upset you last week. Understand that these distractions are totally normal! In the modern world, our brains typically can't stay focused for a longer period.

And this is where the most important aspect of meditation comes in. When your monkey mind jumps from thought to thought, recognize these thoughts without judgment. High achievers will be very critical of themselves at this moment. Why can't I stay still and focused? Why am I thinking of that useless topic from yesterday?

But when your mind begins to wander, take a breath, and notice what's happening without judgment. Don't beat yourself up for it. Your mind will jump around in the early days because it's not used to the "activity of stillness." Don't look for immediate results. Just acknowledge the thought and gradually let it go. Then, bring yourself back to the present moment and the next breath. That's it. You've just meditated. Repeat that process, and you will establish stronger connections with the body and mind.

When you acknowledge a thought, let it go, and center yourself back on breathing, you establish a stronger connection between your body and mind. Like lifting weights, this redirection to the present moment is the "rep." More time in the present moment and bringing your thoughts back to breathing will allow more time in a mindful state.

Like exercise, consistent mindfulness and meditation activities will compound. Over time, you will feel calmer and more present. You will cultivate space between external events and your reaction. You will uncover more depth in your day-to-day activities and creativity in your work.

A consistent mindfulness practice cultivates presence in your relationships, which could offer a richer connection with those you love. You will bring your authentic self more often, and the deep focus will allow peak opportunities of flow state. Sounds great, right? It all starts with the discipline to stay with the practice and embrace the non-doing in the present moment.

The consistent benefits of meditation are vast, and you may be surprised at the number of influential names in business, sports, the arts, and media who all subscribe to a daily meditation practice.[125]

The late Kobe Bryant felt that meditation increased his focus and poise. "I meditate every day. It's like having an anchor. If I don't do it, I feel like I'm constantly chasing the day as opposed to being in control and dictating my day. I am calm about whatever comes my way, a poise that comes from starting my morning with meditation."

Actress Heather Graham discussed how meditation helped calm her anxiety. "I love meditation. I'm high-strung, so getting anxious is easy, but it calms me down. It helps me find that peaceful place inside myself. Whenever life is going a bit crazy, it helps me to be really centered."

Oprah Winfrey established a twice-a-day practice. "I give myself a healthy dose of quiet time at least once (and when I'm on point, twice) a day: twenty minutes in the morning, twenty in the evening. Knowing that stillness is the space where all creative expression, peace, light, and love come to be is a powerfully energizing yet calming experience.

Knowing for sure that even in the daily craziness that bombards us from every direction, there is a constancy of stillness. Only from that space can you create your best work and your best life."

The author Arianna Huffington explains how meditation has added a deeper dimension to her life. "Even if you do, like, ten minutes, it's just a reminder that underneath all of our comings and goings, our successes and our failures, there is a deeper dimension to our lives. We can tap into it and show up from that place, which is wiser, more joyful, more compassionate, and all the things we want more of in our lives."

Billionaire hedge fund manager Ray Dalio has stated that meditation makes him feel like a ninja in a fight in the high-stakes investing game.[126]

The benefits of a consistent meditation practice are vast, helping us explore more profound levels of consciousness to be our most authentic selves. What began as an ancient, mysterious practice is now a mainstream effective tool to create calm, focus, creativity, and a deeper perspective. As the ocean waves of our mind react to the circumstances in the world, we need to pursue still waters to create space for beauty. To get there, we need to embrace the non-doing.

The Talent that Slipped Away

After several months of these constant phone calls and spirit-breaking conversations, my co-worker let everyone off the hook and left the company. However, these types of issues happened to *every* company in our industry, so he encountered them again at his next employer.

I wish I had a different ending for this story, that my inspirational leadership just transformed my co-worker into a ray of positivity. But I learned a long time ago I'm not God, and some things I can't change. Still, I felt sad as I saw my co-worker depart, full of unfulfilled talent and a miserable work experience. In truth, he didn't need to change his surroundings; he needed to change his mindset. A series of decisions—to look for an optimistic path forward, to give grace to others, to appreciate the other positive things in his life, to trust this situation was solvable even though challenging—could have made all the difference. Instead, he chose to defeat, to focus on the thorns instead of the rose.

Maslow's viewpoints on Aesthetic needs remind us that beauty is in the eye of the beholder. Being worried or upset about issues in our modern culture isn't hard; just turn on your social media feed or cable news for an excuse to feel terrible. But strong leaders choose to see the best in others and challenging situations. They focus on how obstacles make us stronger, revealing true beauty and potential in the world and inspiring others to do the same.

Key Themes: Aesthetic

- ➲ Grace, gratitude, optimism, and mindfulness are the four pillars of seeing beauty in the world.
- ➲ Grace recognizes that the forces of good outweigh the forces of evil in the world. Most people try their best, even if they fall short of our expectations. As humans, we will make mistakes but can and will improve.
- ➲ Gratitude is a muscle conditioning your mind to see all that is right in the world. This is not aspirational; it's already present. Better recognition of the good in our lives makes it more likely to see beauty in the future.
- ➲ Optimists have been scientifically proven to achieve more than those with a pessimistic outlook. Optimists may not always know the answer to a challenge but are convinced they will find a way.

⮑ Mindfulness research has exploded in recent years, showing to produce greater calm, focus, creativity, and being more present in our relationships. Having the ability to cultivate stillness in a culture on overdrive can be a superpower.

Maslow's Magic: The Magic in the Application

⮑ Grace: What past mistake or event from yourself or someone else have you been holding onto? Why do you keep replaying it in your mind? Write out how this resentment has held you back from being present.

⮑ The obstacle is the way: look back at one past hardship that turned out to be a blessing in disguise. How did it feel back then? What did you learn that has made you better today?

⮑ List events in the last few years where you rose to a challenge. Now you can have a handy list to reference when telling yourself, "I can do hard things."

⮑ Pick a time each day for the next two weeks to meditate for five to ten minutes. Over time, notice the changes in feeling calm and focused. What would it mean if you could live in a more present state each day?

CHAPTER 8

SELF-ACTUALIZATION
Mindset of a Champion

I stared at the wall wondering what had happened. I had focused my entire life on becoming a professional baseball player, and now I felt like I was sliding backwards. It was the summer between my junior and senior year in college, and I just couldn't hit a baseball anymore. Worse yet, I had wrapped my identity in my performance, so my struggles with hitting were magnified in my personal life. I wasn't just a failing baseball player; I was a worthless human.

As a highly analytical player, I often suffered from analysis paralysis. In baseball, you need to react in milliseconds, so long thoughts are incredibly unhelpful on the playing field. The more I analyzed, the worse I played. Even more frustrating, I would seemingly get it right during practice but failed during game time. I just couldn't let go of the paralyzing thoughts and trust myself.

That summer, I played on a college baseball team in Geneva, NY, with other players from around the country, thinking a little time and space away from my college program would shift my perspective. However, my same struggles only continued. In our locker room early in the season, the manager of the team came to tell me what I could expect for the rest of the season. "McGee, you are going to be the fifth outfielder on this team."

The problem is that only three outfielders play at a time. So, even if one guy got hurt, I still wasn't the next person in. A seismic shift needed to happen if I wanted any meaningful playing time. I thought long and hard about quitting the game and heading home. It just wasn't fun anymore. *Maybe I'm not cut out for this after all,* I thought. *What else am I missing in life?*

Self-Actualization Defined

In Maslow's original theory, self-actualization was the final step in achieving the peak of human potential. Kurt Goldstein, German neurologist and psychiatrist, originally introduced the term. Maslow believed that at this stage, "a new discontent and restlessness will soon develop unless the individual is doing what he is fitted for. A musician must make music, an artist must paint, a poet must write if he is to be ultimately happy. What a man can be, he must be. This need we may call self-actualization."[127]

Self-actualization is the full potential of one's intrinsic, creative, intellectual, and social abilities, where you are performing your best at the things you love most while enjoying the process. You are fully present in what you love and seeing your best shine through.

This stage is unique to any individual with endless possibilities. Sadly, the people who reach this milestone are the exception, not the norm. Maslow noted, "Since, in our society, basically satisfied people are the exception, we do not know much about self-actualization, either experimentally or clinically. It remains a challenging problem for research." This isn't surprising considering our divisive society with high levels of depression and anxiety, which has kept the self-help industry growing exponentially.

So, why do so few people achieve this level of self-actualization? In the original model, this state is achieved only if we fully engage with previous needs like health, safety, love, esteem, creativity, and beauty. To operate at your best, you have a lot of variables to consider. How can you optimize those needs to perform at your best most frequently?

Power of Habit: A Precursor to Flow?

Maslow originally hypothesized that a person must meet the lower, basic needs to operate in a peak state, causing a significant amount cognitive stress for anyone trying to function at their best.

Do you lack the willpower or effort? Do you want it bad enough? What about the long series of checklists you go through while you stare at the mirror and brush your teeth in the morning? The immense workload and mental stress to meet all these needs would make it nearly impossible to accomplish daily. Paralysis by analysis would set in.

Any highly fulfilled individual's success didn't come by chance or fate. They are not overwhelmed by a massive checklist of "all the things I have to do" to live in a self-actualized state. By definition, self-actualizers are more likely to have established the lower-level needs of physiology, belongingness, security, esteem, creativity, and aesthetics. Scientists call this phenomenon "cognitive load." Cognitive load is similar to how much RAM you use on your computer; the only difference is that the "computer" is the human brain.

The more tasks we give it, the more likely it is to slow down. However, the best self-actualizers only think about their previous needs occasionally. In fact, they think about them a little less. Self-actualizers have established habit systems in the lower levels to allow them to focus on the activities they enjoy the most. They spend more time in self-actualization because they have created routines establishing base-level needs.

High achievers have created automated systems to meet lower-end needs, freeing up creative energy to pursue their passionate pursuits. According to James Clear, these systems come from a consistent, intentional focus on doing the work to operate at their best.

James Clear is the author of the bestselling book *Atomic Habits*, a weekly newsletter, and a speaker at major companies and events. He has dedicated his life to mastering the small art of improving each day, which separates the truly elite from the average. His work is fascinating from both a science and simplicity standpoint, and can help you focus on what's most important. The work described in this passage is taken from *Atomic Habits*, along with Clear's website and other writings.[128]

According to Clear, we become who we think we are. While an initial burst of motivation may help you start the critical work, this spark will often fizzle over time. People who stick with habits tend to do so because the routine becomes part of their identity. Research shows that when people believe in an aspect of their identity, their actions align with said belief.

Let's say the goal is to lose weight. We live in a complicated minefield of unhealthy choices trying to derail you. When forced to find a snack out of the house, you may look for a healthy, convenient option. You might look for the Snickers bar sitting conveniently beneath the counter of the local convenience store.

But if you have the identity of a healthy person, you will work a little harder to comb the aisles and hunt down raw almonds. Or take time before leaving the house to pack a healthy snack so you won't be in that situation in the first place. Those actions align with your identity as a healthy person. Choosing the healthy option isn't rocket science, but requires a series of disciplined actions leading to the desired result (and identity) of who you are...a healthy person.

Clear also gives an excellent plane analogy for the power of habit. If a plane is flying from Los Angeles to New York City, and the pilot adjusts the aircraft by just 3.5 degrees during takeoff, the plane would end up in Washington, DC, instead of New York. You wouldn't notice this adjustment when the plane took off; it would feel like you were heading in the same direction. But given that slight adjustment and enough flight time, you would end up hundreds of miles from your intended destination. The exact analogy relates to our tiny daily habits which accumulate into our best selves.

Why Habits Fail

It seems so easy. But clearly, something keeps us from doing what we know needs to be done. An overwhelming number of New Year's resolutions ultimately fail, so why is it so hard to stick with positive habits? According to Clear, there are five ways habits can ultimately fail.

Problem 1: Trying to Change Everything at Once

Pursuing self-actualization will take a lifetime; it's impossible to perform all the necessary behavior changes simultaneously.

Clear recommends only focusing on three new habits at a time in order to establish a routine and make them more automatic. After they become ingrained, you can take on other behaviors to layer into the person you want to become.

Choose a keystone habit. Sometimes one habit can trigger for the rest of your habits. Maybe you choose to go to bed early so you can wake energized for your day. Or maybe you start exercising, which will make you second guess your diet because you don't want to negate the work you've done. Or maybe you start having family dinner four times each week to build relationships with your family.

Problem 2: Starting with a Habit That is Too Big

If you choose a challenging habit to achieve, you will probably regress into old habits. If you want to start a meditation practice, start with one minute daily. Choosing a simple, easy, and manageable habit will help you do it again the next time. When one minute of meditating becomes easy, up the time frame.

Problem 3: Seeking a Result, Not a Ritual

Nick Saban, head football coach at the University of Alabama, is famous for his approach to success called "The Process." Despite winning more national championships than any collegiate football coach, he doesn't obsess about the trophy. Instead, Saban focuses on the components of a winning team (recruiting, nutrition, coaching leadership, academic support, etc.). His emphasis on what causes success allows his team to shine on the field.

Problem 4: Not Changing Your Environment

Accomplishing your goal is easier if your environment isn't holding you back. If you are in the Love/Belongingness stage and looking to build an inclusive team, don't allow toxic people to linger. Or, if you want to lose weight, don't fill your pantry with enticing snack foods, quickly capitalizing on your weary mind when blood sugar is low. If you are trying to quit drinking, don't take a job as a bartender.

Problem 5: Assuming Small Changes Don't Add Up

Saving $5,000 this year has a nice ring to it. Thinking about saving that much certainly gets you excited! But do you have the same excitement for saving $96 per week? Probably not so much. But the $96 per week over time will help you reach your goal.

Your focus should be on growing one percent better each day. Yes, this growth is small, but attainable, and it most definitely adds up. If you grow one percent better each day, you will be 37 times better over a year. It's amazing what a little progress can do over time.

So, build the behaviors to succeed first, and the results will follow. As Nick Saban reminds us, it's all about the process.

Why Habits Work

James Clear lays the systems for developing strong habits out in a very, well, "clear" way. Think of habit formation as the loop of four stages: cue, craving, response, and reward.

A cue triggers your brain to initiate a behavior. It can be a signal of information that predicts a reward. An alarm clock. A buzz on your phone. A growling stomach. The smell of roasted coffee beans as you walk by a coffee shop. All of these things are triggers for a future reward.

Cravings are the motivational force behind every habit. How does this action make me feel? How will it change my state? Every craving is linked to a desire for a new feeling. Smokers don't crave the cigarette but the ensuing relief smoking provides. We don't get excited about turning on the TV but we want to be entertained. Runners don't look forward to pounding the pavement but rather the explosive euphoria of "runner's high" accompanying exercise. The response is the practical action following the cue and craving.

Are you longing for connection and love? The response could be hugging your loved one. Craving a sense of beauty? The answer is taking a nature walk and paying attention to the sounds.

You will only act if you feel like the craving will be satisfied by your action, but make sure you begin with an easier action in order to follow through. If I have a passion for pizza, I can easily order one from my phone while I sit stagnant on the couch. The best marketers know customers will follow suit if you make something easy to buy.

The final step is the reward. The reward is the end goal of the habit and has two components to it. First, it satisfies a craving and teaches and gives us feedback. Getting a promotion can provide more money or respect. Drinking water provides energy for survival. However temporary, the rewards are satisfying, delivering contentment and relief from craving.

Second, the reward demonstrates how to behave in the future. Have you had a craving for barbecue and satisfied it at the local smokehouse? You might notice a significant drop in energy an hour later. This fatigue reveals that you shouldn't eat this meal before a big presentation. Or perhaps you see a positive response from your team after surprising them with a fun, offsite team-building event in the afternoon. This excitement reveals your team desires connection and building cultural bonds.

Let's give a simple, modern-day example of how this could work. Your phone buzzes on the table (cue). You want to learn what the message says (craving).

You interrupt your current work and pick up your phone (response). You satisfy your craving for information (reward). It's alarming how many people's physiological response changes when their phone buzzes, showing how habituated these systems can become.

To create a good habit, we need to lower any roadblocks to good behaviors. For a cue, make it obvious. For the craving, make it attractive. The response needs to be easy to capitalize on the craving. And the reward needs to be satisfying to condition the brain to frequently repeat this habit.

Let's try building an exercise habit. Perhaps we set the alarm clock in the morning when we have no distractions and haven't started the day (cue). While getting out of bed, we're thinking about the energy following our work out, which will catapult us from our current, groggy state. We make it easy to find our workout gear because we've packed our bags, and they're waiting by the door (response). We celebrate by logging our workout output in a journal charting our progress (reward).

However, in order to build positive feedback systems, we must eliminate negative habits blocking our way. To reduce the likelihood of repeating bad habits, do the opposite of the bad habit. We need to make the cues invisible and the craving unattractive.

Let's look at a few examples of bad habits we are trying to break. When the cue comes, we need to make the habit invisible. Imagine you are trying to lose ten pounds. One way to make the habit invisible is to eliminate all unhealthy snack foods in your pantry. Not having junk food in your environment removes the need for a bad habit.

The second step is to make the craving unattractive. People trying to reduce screen time usage may charge their phones outside their bedrooms at night. This relocation reduces the chance you hear the buzzing of a notification and the subsequent urge to pick it up. It also creates more work for you to leave bed to get your phone, especially in the middle of the night. All of this added work will make it difficult (and not necessarily rewarding) to scroll at all hours of the night.

Want a healthy body? Establish the identity of a healthy person and set your alarm clock for 5 am to exercise. Want healthy connections with your teams? Establish regular check-in times on your calendar to understand how your team members feel. Want creative output on your projects? Establish regular design thinking sessions for your teams to brainstorm new concepts and take risks on novel ideas.

You can apply this system to any scenario, but we must make the lower-level needs automatic, which is obviously easier said than done, as we frequently bounce around the hierarchy to meet the day's most pressing needs and challenges. But, over time, many key components to a self-actualized career will become habit and commonplace. With your lower-level needs met you can fully enter one of Maslow's peak states.

Entering Flow State

Athletes may call it "in the zone." Locked in. Musicians may call it "in the pocket." Runners might call it a "runner's high". Many terms exist to describe flow state. It feels euphoric, like we are in a spiritual or religious moment.

Many of us felt our best and unstoppable during moments of flow state. We are calm but focused and excited. Fully immersed and present in our activity. We are operating at our best and showcasing great work. We don't need external rewards because we do it for ourselves as we follow our purpose.

For most people, flow state feels like a fleeting moment; a rare but glorious time when we are joyful and experiencing our best. The basketball player may feel "on fire" as they drill seven straight three-point shots. The salesperson may give a client the perfect pitch. A presentation you prepared on a passionate topic brings out your best self on stage. An artist works in the wee hours of the morning, immersed in their masterpiece.

You are not thinking about yesterday's disappointments or tomorrow's worries or who might judge you. You are locked in, doing the work. These moments can often define us over our lifetime, the culmination of all we are and can become.

The flow state can be an overwhelming but rare experience. I'm pretty sure if a pharmaceutical company created a drug called "flow state," it would be the greatest-selling drug of all time. But how can we bottle up these flow-state opportunities to experience them more often? Luckily for us, flow states aren't just catching lightning in a bottle or experiencing the freak nature of these peak states. There is a science to this euphoric state; we can explore those states' elements of self-actualization.

So, how do we define such a state? Mihaly Csikszentmihalyi is one of the earliest pioneers in flow science and explains it is "a state in which people are so involved in an activity that nothing else seems to matter; the experience is so enjoyable that people will continue to do it even at great cost, for the sheer sake of doing it."[129]

Flow state is the feeling of seeking enjoyment over short-term happiness when engaged in an activity which balances skill and challenges, clear goals, and immediate feedback. We forget our flaws and focus on the intrinsic rewards of learning and improving. We release our self-consciousness and concept of time, gaining a high level of concentration and absorption in the task at hand. We are seeking something money, status, and prestige doesn't offer. We have a high sense of focus and control.

The flow state is where action and awareness merge. We become one with our activity, and our efforts feel automatic. We lose our sense of self, and the inner critic is silenced. We lose track of time, becoming fully present. Although we are appropriately challenged, in many ways, we feel effortless.

Flow state is a spectrum experience. You may encounter "microflow" when experiencing some, but not all, of the states above, which can feel like a momentary burst of enlightenment. Conversely, we can experience "macroflow" when all the above characteristics appear.

While we most often experience individual flow states, we can also experience group flow in a team setting. The University of North

Carolina psychologist Keith Sawyer has written on this topic and describes several triggers that can spark group flow.[130]

Groups in flow have shared goals and closely listen to one another. Remember the "yes, and" exercise from Maslow's cognitive needs? Instead of debating ideas, they build on each other's ideas. The group is fully present and operates with control. They blend egos and ensure everyone is contributing. The group is in constant communication, connecting with easy familiarity. Lastly, they all have some skin in the game and assume shared risk for the outcomes. So how do we get to this magical state of flow? And if so, why can't we get there more often?

Steven Kotler, bestselling author of eleven books with flow as a central theme, is the founder of The Flow Research Collective, an organization devoted to the research and application of flow state. He is one of the foremost modern thought leaders on the science and application of flow state. His work is an excellent place to start for those wanting to learn more. As a primer, we will highlight many of Kotler's analyses below.[131]

Per Kotler's work, no agreed-upon neurobiological definition of flow exists. He believes it aligns with a decrease in brain activity in the prefrontal cortex, or what some refer to as transient hypofrontality. This decrease in brain activity is actually an efficiency exchange. Because flow demands a high level of focus, it trades energy generally used for other things and reallocates it for attention, which explains why we have a heightened sense of awareness and feel locked in.

We also see a change in neurochemistry as a combination of norepinephrine, dopamine, endorphins, anandamide, serotonin, and even oxytocin explodes into the system. While these chemicals may not appear in all flow states, they cause a significant rush which feels like a deeply spiritual experience.

So, what prevents most people from reaching these optimum states? From Mihaly Csikszentmihalyi's perspective, most people seek short-term happiness over longer-term enjoyment, or better described, longer-term fulfillment. Put in other terms, we work harder to fulfill short-term needs with instant gratification rather than delight in a more time-consuming and difficult pursuit that can be deeply fulfilling. TV, the internet, your social media feed, and a cocktail at the end of the workday might all satisfy short-term needs but will never allow us to enter deeper states of fulfillment.

Our minds seek the path of least resistance in an attempt to escape from the anxieties of the modern world. While this easy fix might solve an immediate need, it doesn't allow us to reach the higher levels of consciousness we experience in the flow state.

For many, the flow state might feel like a surprise visitor who comes and goes as they please. It simply appears without notice or warning. However, Kotler and other flow researchers believe certain triggers can drive individuals to reach flow more consistently, which in turn causes our performance and fulfillment to skyrocket.

According to Kotler, there are four flow triggers. The first trigger is complete concentration in the present moment. This present mindset allows the prefrontal cortex to down-regulate and deploy its energy on your creative pursuits. The practice of mindfulness can be a great bridge to the focus and calm necessary to a flow state.

The next flow trigger is taking part in a goal with immediate feedback. The cause-and-effect gap is small, so we can make tiny adjustments to fine-tune our skills over time. These micro-adjustments will compound (like a healthy habit system) to reach your desired goal faster.

The third trigger is setting clear goals. More than just the end state of a goal, like winning a basketball game, we can chunk our clear goals down into smaller, even more clear micro-goals describing each step of the journey. If you play basketball, your clear goal could be shooting ten free throws in a row which puts you in a better position to win the game—or maybe, it would be having the lowest number of turnovers in the game.

The last trigger is placing yourself in a position that stretches your skills but doesn't overwhelm you. In 1908, psychologists Robert Yerkes and John Dodson discovered an empirical relationship between stress (challenge) and performance (see the following sample graph).[132] Flow occurs in the sweet spot between challenge and performance.

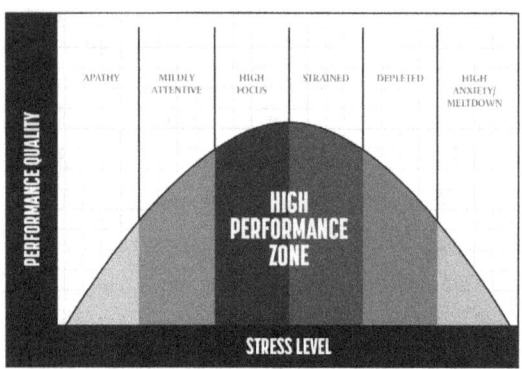

With more research, we'll understand more about this mystical flow state, but for now, we have a basic framework for experiencing a flow state more often. When we align with our passions and live purposefully, we will have more ability to operate in these peak experiences.

The Buddha and a Baseball

I thought long and hard about quitting baseball that summer and just enjoying my senior year in college as a regular student, but I knew the what-ifs and regret would eat at me. I decided to continue with the summer league and do my best as a role player coming off the bench. My mission was to enjoy this final calendar year of my baseball career before I moved on to the real world.

During that summer, I began to research mindfulness. I needed something to calm my mind and increase focus in the moment. I read a number of books and was particularly interested in Phil Jackson's work with the Chicago Bulls, ultimately beginning a practice of mindfulness each day. For me, mindfulness meant paying close attention to my breath using some of the previously mentioned exercises, for a set period each day. I began a routine and started to sense a shift; I was more calm, more present, more focused, and more creative. As this daily ritual became habit, I realized I was no longer lamenting the past or worrying about the future; I was right here, right now, enjoying the moment.

In the middle of that summer season, other things began to shift on the team. Through a combination of a few injuries, lineup rotations, and other hitters entering their own slump, I had a chance to play again. This time, however, was much different. I was more calm, focused, and relaxed. Trusting myself. It was the exact opposite of what I had felt only a month earlier.

Surprisingly, my performance made a 180-degree turn. Despite not trying to "achieve" anything with mindfulness outside of simply being present, my performance took off. I went from being one of the worst hitters on the team to one of the best. The coach started writing my name in the lineup card regularly as the leadoff hitter and starting centerfielder. It was a dramatic twist I hadn't anticipated.

That summer was one of my most magical seasons. I lived with a wonderful host family, met a number of new friends who played at colleges throughout the country, and saw my performance rise to a new personal peak at the college level. Our team made an improbable rally at the end of the season to win the championship in the Northeast Collegiate Baseball League, and I still have the ring to prove it. I will never forget that summer, one that restored my childlike joy for a game I loved.

When I returned to Seton Hall for my senior season, I was a completely different player and person. My mindset had shifted, my habits changed, and my performance was elevated. My summer success continued into my senior year at Seton Hall, and I was named a team captain. I continued to hit first in the starting lineup, playing centerfield, leading the team in stolen bases, and being one of the best hitters on the team.

My mindfulness habits freed up my cognitive load to operate more frequently within flow states, which significantly improved my performance. I finished my season feeling like I had played my best without an ounce of regret. In June, the Major League Baseball draft came and went, but I wasn't selected. While I had brief contact with a couple of professional teams after the draft, nothing materialized; my competitive baseball career was over.

While some people might enter a deep depression when their childhood dream doesn't materialize, I had a different perspective. I had discovered the principles to unlock my highest performance levels. While not talented enough to play professionally, I could leave my baseball career knowing I was a good college player who left it all out on the field. Without any regrets, I was able to peacefully close a chapter of my life and look forward to a business profession ahead.

My mindfulness habits have spilled over into my professional life, becoming a mainstay. Despite my sometimes-overactive brain, my colleagues tell me I exude a calm, even-keeled confidence. The by-products of mindfulness—peacefulness, clarity, focus, creativity—all translate when I'm engaging with my colleagues and working on complex problems. Now, that's not to say I live in a 24-hour state of golden bliss. Far from it! But I *am* able to more easily reorient myself back to the present moment when things inevitably go awry.

Abraham Maslow recognized that for humans to operate closer to their peak potential, they must establish their lower level needs to free up space for their higher-level pursuits. Self-actualization cannot be achieved without this foundation. Aristotle said, "We are what we repeatedly do. Therefore, excellence is not an act, but a habit."

Ask yourself: What are the necessary habits to be your best as a person and leader? Physical health habits? Relational habits to develop more connectivity? Mental habits to think creatively about new problems to solve?

In today's environment of information overload, distractions can feel like mental warfare. Leaders cannot possibly react to every shred of information, instead we need to be intentional with how we use our time and focus. How can we stay disciplined to repeatedly do the important things so they become natural? How do we free up time and space so we can experience a flow state?

Key Themes: Self-Actualization

➲ The power of solid habits can be a vital precursor to flow state.
➲ Strong habits will automate the necessary lower needs while freeing up cognitive capacity to immerse yourself in the present moment.
➲ The most common flow triggers are present-moment awareness, immediate feedback, and clear goals. In addition, you can reach a flow state when our skills are stretched but not overwhelmed.
➲ Groups can also experience a flow state. Groups can enter a flow state by sharing, closely listening to each other, being fully present, blending egos, having a high sense of control, and assuming shared risk in the outcome.

Maslow's Magic: The Magic in the Application

➲ What is one habit that would significantly improve the quality of your life? What can you do to make it easier to establish this habit?

⮩ How can you help drive group flow? Write out a paragraph on how you can create a shared set of team goals so everyone has skin in the game. As a leader, what can you do to make them feel in control? Can you commit to giving small but immediate feedback so the team can make micro-adjustments in real time?

CHAPTER 9

TRANSCENDENCE
A Higher Calling

If only there were a way to slow down the rotation of the Earth; that would solve the problem! Slowing down the Earth's rotation could elongate our days, allowing us more time to focus on everything we'd like to do. I can't tell you how many days I would have liked more time. Perhaps this is another moonshot opportunity for the great minds of Silicon Valley, or maybe we shouldn't give them any ideas!

Driving home after my first week as a new Product Manager, I asked myself if I was making a mistake. While this product launch was exciting, it was going to consume every ounce of me. I had to learn so much—and quickly. Within the first week, I was meeting my new colleagues in product marketing, regulatory affairs, digital marketing, supply chain, R&D, and finance. As a former sales manager, I didn't have much experience with these different functions. While meeting new people and learning about their jobs was exciting, I realized how differently I would need to think and operate with new stakeholders. Since there was no blueprint for this launch and we had never done anything remotely close to this before, we had to figure it out as we went.

How on earth can I figure this out quickly? I wondered. Even more pressing was my situation at home. I had two children under the age of 4, and my very pregnant wife would be delivering our third child in the next few months. So much for perfect timing with life and career! The demands on my presence and time would be amplified both at work and at home. The expectations as an employee, husband, and father would be crushing when layered on top of one another. *If we could only slow down the Earth's rotation.*

Then, like a light bulb over a cartoon character, a distant memory popped into my mind. "I need to build a Guiding Coalition around me!" I knew the only way to accomplish the organization's big goals would be mobilizing an army of willing lieutenants who could accomplish what one man couldn't do alone.

The idea of a Guiding Coalition arrived in the form of a presentation three years prior. Our company was about to endure a different organizational change process, and our VP of Sales invited Dr. John Kotter, an author and professor from nearby Harvard Business School, to speak to our front-line sales leaders. Dr. Kotter detailed his change management process, which included building a Guiding Coalition to drive the change throughout the organization. I love frameworks, but could Dr. Kotter's process unlock opportunity for our team? Could it alleviate the demands on the Product Managers to do it alone? Could it help me navigate an extraordinarily pressure-filled season of my life?

Transcendence in the Workforce

Conventional thinking on Maslow's hierarchy usually stops at self-actualization, which makes the final destination, transcendence, even more fascinating.

Even Maslow himself considered self-actualization the final summit for human development until the last years of his life. Despite the massive success of the original theory of motivational needs, Maslow was restless with the finality of it and was willing to debunk his original theory in pursuit of a higher calling.

Despite achieving all of one's personal capabilities and becoming deeply fulfilled in the process, self-actualization seems limited. How does your performance and fulfillment have a lasting effect on others and the world around you? Maslow realized you needed a transcendent spirit to fully recognize your human potential.

"Transcendence refers to the very highest and most inclusive or holistic levels of human consciousness, behaving and relating, as ends rather than means, to oneself, to significant others, to human beings in general, to other species, to nature, and to the cosmos," writes Maslow.[133]

Scott Barry Kaufmann has extensively studied Maslow and summarizes transcendence quite well.[134] "Healthy transcendence is an emergent phenomenon resulting from the harmonious integration of one's whole self in the service of cultivating the good society." Kaufmann continues to explain that, "healthy transcendence involves harnessing all that you are in the service of realizing the best version of yourself so you can help raise the bar for the whole of humanity."

In a world obsessed with self-image, self-care, and self-everything else, transcendence elevates our primary purpose above our personal needs and ego to pursue a higher calling. Maslow appropriately named this higher calling, "peak experiences."

While Maslow's work was a motivational theory and not a rigorous study, other research supports the need for transcendence in the modern-day leader.

Maslow's work and description of transcendence show a striking similarity to what bestselling author Jim Collins calls "Level 5 leadership."

Level 5 leaders ascend a similar pyramid hierarchy as depicted in Maslow's theory. In Collins's perennial bestselling book *Good to Great*, Collins highlights the top-performing 11 companies out of 1,435, appearing on the Fortune 500 list over 30 years. In all 11, a "Level 5 leader" was present.[135]

So, what is a Level 5 leader? Collins's describes it with this statement:[136]

> "Level 5 leaders display a powerful mixture of personal humility and indomitable will. They're incredibly ambitious, but their ambition is first and foremost for the *cause*, for the organization and its purpose, not themselves. While Level 5 leaders can come in many personality packages, they are often self-effacing, quiet, reserved, and even shy. Every good-to-great transition in our research began with a Level 5 leader who motivated the enterprise more with inspired standards than inspiring personality.

The business world contains many examples of how the pursuit of self-gain through self-actualization alone has been limiting for humanity. Who can forget the stories of Enron, WorldCom, AIG, Adelphia, and Tyco at the turn of the century? In each saga, executives' pursuit of profit for its own sake created havoc for the company, their customers, shareholders, and the world around them.[137] Clearly, these leaders had yet to hit the Level 5 Summit and the spirit of transcendence.

Try to imagine the pressure business leaders are under. Particularly in Western societies, businesses are rewarded for growing their revenues and profits, and it might be easy to overlook some human fundamentals when running a business. Cut a corner here, fudge the result there.

With so much money on the line, some leaders may be tempted to participate in self-serving behavior. Capitalism as a system has been a significant driver of the technological innovation of the 20th and 21st centuries. Unlike socialism, capitalism is a world where capital markets operate freely with minimal government involvement. When individuals and companies are highly incentivized to produce value in the marketplace, they experience increased innovation, problem-solving, and financial rewards.

And like a growing wave, success begets more success.

No other system in the world has done more to pull up the standard of living for the average citizen and lift people out of poverty. Of course everyone isn't a winner in the game of capitalism, but net-net, more people in Western society have benefited from this system than socialism.

But too much of a good thing can happen. When greed and the pursuit of profits for our own means overwhelm other societal responsibilities, chaos can ensue.

Capitalism Drives Western Values

Particularly in Western cultures, we see how modern-day capitalism has influenced our corporate and personal values. Capitalism is both criticized and celebrated politically, making the U.S. the world's economic engine.

Capitalism is defined as an economic and political system in which private owners control a country's trade and industry for profit rather than by the state. Simple enough. But the execution and beneficiaries of that system has differed throughout time. Let's consider two variations of capitalism.

Adam Smith was an 18th-century Scottish philosopher commonly known as the father of economics and modern capitalism who wrote *The Wealth of Nations*. In it, he said that "Consumption is the sole end and purpose of all production and the interest of the producer ought to be attended to, only so far as it may be necessary for promoting that of the consumer."[138]

So, in Adam Smith's definition of capitalism, the consumer was king. Producers were present to provide value for the consumer, not vice versa.

Even so, companies or producers did have their self-preservation in mind. Every company wants to be the best at something; they want to make the best product, good, or service which brings the most value to their customer. And the consumer still wins by receiving great products and services at competitive prices. For many years, this definition of capitalism worked well for all stakeholders, which included bondholders, customers, employees, communities, and suppliers.

This early form of capitalism created an ecosystem effect, causing more significant value than just the sum of its parts. For example, when Henry Ford profited from scaling the modern-day supply chain, so did the various suppliers of automobile components, employees with lifetime pension checks, etc. This ecosystem effect is how a rising tide lifts all boats.

But in the 1970s, something more perverse happened in modern business. Milton Friedman, a professor at the University of Chicago, issued a scathing response to this "stakeholder" approach to modern capitalism.

In a famous essay penned for *The New York Times*, Friedman mocked the modern approach:

I am reminded of the wonderful line about the Frenchman who discovered at the age of 70 that he had been speaking prose all his life. The businessmen believe that they are defending free enterprise when they declaim that business is not concerned "merely" with profit but also with promoting desirable "social" ends; that business has a "social conscience" and takes seriously its responsibilities for providing employment, eliminating discrimination, avoiding pollution and whatever else may be the catchwords of the contemporary crop of reformers. In fact they are—or would be if they or anyone else took them seriously—preaching pure and unadulterated socialism. Businessmen who talk this way are unwitting puppets of the intellectual forces that have been undermining the basis of a free society these past decades.

Friedman believed the sole purpose of business is to produce profits for its owners. He wrapped up the article with this quote, "there is one and only one social responsibility of business—to use its resources and engage in activities designed to increase its profits so long as it stays within the rules of the game, which is to say, engages in open and free competition without deception or fraud."[139] From Friedman's perspective, as long as you make money ethically, you win the game of business.

Unfortunately, this motivation took hold of Western business in the 1970s and 1980s, epitomized by the Gordon Gecko figure in the movie Wall Street from 1987. Businesses focused more on reaching short-term figures in earnings reports rather than building long-lasting healthy companies.

The world has witnessed too many painful episodes of this singular approach to shareholder supremacy at the expense of all other stakeholders. Some examples include mass layoffs by thousands of companies, Enron blatantly manipulating financial documents to please short-term earnings reports, or B.P. spilling oil over weeks into the Gulf of Mexico.

You can also see examples in sports where individuals or groups cut corners on their values to achieve short-term success. Lance Armstrong lied to the sports world and cancer community about his blood doping involvement when he won a record 7 Tour de France championships. Barry Bonds, Sammy Sosa, and Mark McGwire all took performance-enhancing drugs in their pursuit of home run glory in Major League Baseball.

And how did this work out for them? Despite their impressive statistics, Armstrong was stripped of his Tour de France victories, and Bonds, Sosa, and McGwire have yet to be inducted into the MLB Hall of Fame. When groups or individuals pursue their own gain and don't consider their stakeholders, everyone loses.

A Glimmer of Hope

Fortunately, modern-day business has a glimmer of hope. Under pressure from political and social leaders and emerging personal convictions, many business leaders are beginning to align their business purpose and responsibility.

The Business Roundtable, an organization of CEOs from some of the largest and most successful U.S. companies was formed in 1972. Since then, their goal has been to promote a thriving economy and expand opportunities for all Americans through sound public policy. The B.R. works closely with members of both political parties to create an environment that benefits job creation, opportunity, and competition in the U.S. marketplace.

Recognizing the negative, unintended consequences from the "profits over everything" mindset in U.S. business, the Business Roundtable worked together to form a new definition of the role of the U.S. corporation, stating they have a fundamental commitment to: delivering value to customers, investing in employees, dealing fairly and ethically with suppliers, supporting the communities in which they work, and generating long-term value for stakeholders.

This commitment means it's not all gloom and doom, and hope exists. At least some of these leaders understand the broader ecosystem when defining their business's purpose. Of course, tension will always exist between meeting financial commitments and doing what's right. After all, companies have to make money or they won't be around for too long.

But everyone can benefit when businesses begin to look at building a foundation set to benefit more stakeholders over a longer time.

Corporate Social Responsibility

The idea of Corporate Social Responsibility, or CSR, is emerging from the stakeholder capitalism perspective. Companies typically track activities in a CSR program internally. They can include activities like lowering a business's carbon footprint, corporate volunteering, improving workforce practices, and engaging in charitable endeavors. For example, CSR could be Microsoft working to lower its carbon footprint and Verizon providing technology to school children to reduce the digital divide.

Environmental, Social, and Governance

For some time, people considered CSR the philanthropic arm of a company focused on social benefits, but it needed help tracking its quantitative impact on business performance. In response to the uncertainty over authentic business results, CSR evolved into the adoption of Environmental, Social, and Governance programs (ESG) to track and measure results. The big question is: Can companies prove they can perform well by being good?

ESG strategies have become deeply embedded in many companies' value-creation models. In a 2020 McKinsey report, 83 percent of C-suite leaders and investors believed ESG programs would create more shareholder value in a five-year period. These metrics were quantifiable and showcased for investors.

Proponents of ESG programs indicate visible benefits in more top-line growth as new market segments are created. Cost reductions can occur by eliminating water and carbon impact. Regulatory relief can be present with less governmental pressure and more community support. Productivity can increase with more motivated employees who feel aligned to the organization's values. And lastly, investments and asset optimization towards more ESG-centric opportunities can improve a company's overall financial picture.

Some companies are doing ESG well and getting meaningful results. However, other companies have taken advantage of ESG programs by using it as a marketing campaign to attract eco-conscious stakeholders, but don't deliver on their commitments.

One good example of false ESG was State Street, which built the "Fearless Girl" statue within the NYC financial district as a sign of female empowerment; a signal of the firm's mission to provide a more inclusive workforce and promote equal opportunity.[140] However, at the same time, State Street also agreed to pay $5 million to resolve a federal investigation into whether it discriminated against female and black executives by paying them less than their counterparts. Was the Fearless Girl a cover for more systemic issues within the business at State Street? Was she simply a symbol to attract investors who wanted serve the common good yet failing to live up to that promise within the company?

On the flip side, let's look at a positive example from CVS Caremark. In 2014, CVS stopped selling cigarettes and other tobacco-related products at its stores, since it didn't align with its underlying mission to improve health. This decision resulted in an immediate $2 billion LOSS for the company and the company was mocked by investment experts on Wall Street.

Yes, the firm's stock price did fall one percent the following day, from $66.11 to $65.44. However, as the company transformed its mission and attracted more principal-driven investors and suppliers, the stock rocketed to $113.65 a year and a half after the announcement.

The best part about the CVS story was that customers who formerly purchased cigarettes at their stores didn't just show up somewhere else to get their nicotine fix. In the areas where CVS had a higher market share cigarette sales decreased and the number of nicotine patch sales increased.

Although it resulted in a slight short-term stock price reduction, CVS's decision resulted in a longer-term financial win for the company and community health. With the definition of success beginning to shift, we can be inspired that it is possible to be good by doing good.

CSR and ESG are here to stay and, if done appropriately, can aid the Business Roundtable's goals of building a more sustainable ecosystem of stakeholder capitalism. While ESG storylines can be inspiring, a transcendent leader will demand positive results for all stakeholders.

Driving Change

Maslow's ideas of transcendence in the workforce are becoming possible as the business world values companies pursuing the common good. Companies are rushing to develop leaders who espouse these same values.

Once a leader's values and purpose align, they can take on the final summit of transcendence. This summit is where the rubber meets the road, separating those who talk a big game and those who deliver results, which can challenge the most adept leaders in a fast-moving, complex world. Transcendent leaders need to drive change in their companies and the markets they disrupt.

As mentioned in this chapter's opening, one of the foremost authors on Change Management in the U.S. is John Kotter, a former professor at Harvard Business School and author of several books on driving change, leadership, and executing strategy in modern organizations. His insights and wisdom on how successful leaders drive change within their organizations captivated me.

Kotter is best known for his eight steps to change formula, and we will explore the role of the leader in each stage:[141]

1. Create a Sense of Urgency
2. Build a Guiding Coalition
3. Form a Strategic Vision
4. Enlist a Volunteer Army
5. Enable Action by Removing Barriers
6. Generate Short-Term Wins
7. Sustain Acceleration
8. Institute Change: Make it Stick

Create a Sense of Urgency:

Every company's significant change moment starts with a spark. A new, unexpected competitor has entered the business. A competitor may be going out of business. Or a new technological development in another industry has cross-over appeal for your line of work. Or a war breaks out in Europe, threatening global supply chains. Whatever the pending event, our leaders feel a sense of urgency to act. But how do we create the same urgency within our organization?

First, remember that people act based on the thought of losing something or the thrill of gaining something. In a fast-moving economy, we risk being lapped by our competitors as new opportunities emerge every day out of the blue. Leaders need to inspire people to pursue a bold, aspirational opportunity.

For our new product launch, we created a sense of urgency by pushing two pressing issues, one daunting and one transformative. On one hand, our low-cost competitors would be rushing to attack our legacy product portfolio, trying to commoditize it. On the other hand, this new product line had the opportunity to create a $100 million new surgical category, truly separating us from the competition, transforming hospital processes for kidney stone procedures, and creating a new market.

A sense of urgency can excite people who want to build a compelling vision together. To get someone's attention, we need to spark a business opportunity or solve a challenge...now!

We can't wait a minute longer.

Build a Guiding Coalition:

With excitement building and the desire to act, we need to recruit our guiding coalition. This leadership team will comprise team members who support the cause and have time, skills, and influence to execute this change. These individuals work with high initiative and collaboration, acting urgently as a megaphone for new ideas.

For our guiding coalition, we established a core team who would focus on this opportunity. Each function elected a leader to support the broader launch. Each country elected a marketing representative to participate in global planning activities and synthesize those findings for their local markets. In the U.S. sales organization, we had a small tribe of strategic product specialists to assist the first customers onboard the new product line and train our field sales team.

The guiding coalition must also want to impact something greater than themselves and are aspiring Level 5 leaders. Building the right team of individuals on your guiding coalition is essential to exponentially moving the business.

Form a Strategic Vision:

A strategic vision is the optimal end-state of our change project. How does the firm capitalize on the opportunity to make it a reality? What does the end-game look like? What are the steps to get there? These questions all need to be solved in the strategic vision.

When I first saw Kotter's model, vision as the third step of the change process surprised me. Wouldn't conventional wisdom state it should go first? Isn't vision what gets people excited?

But taking a step back, Kotter's order makes complete sense. To execute a vision, you need to get others to believe in that vision on the front end. By establishing your guiding coalition before the vision stage, your early-stage recruits have a say in the end-game. If people buy in and contribute to defining success, they are more engaged and motivated to see it through.

Our vision was clear: we were the surgical leader for kidney stone disease, and innovation in our field depended on us. Nobody else was innovating like we we were, and we had a responsibility to our customers and patient care to move the field forward. It wasn't just good for business; it was good for humanity.

Enlist a Volunteer Army:

Once you have a sense of urgency for necessary change, your guiding coalition in place, and a clear and compelling vision, you must recruit the volunteer army. These individuals will be executing the work, so they need to buy into the mission's purpose and seek to identify with the project. Clearly remembering what's in it for the business (your vision) but also communicating to the volunteer army what's in it for them individually is critical.

In any new product launch, we always see the top 20 percent of the field sales organization getting out fast, making new discoveries, and understanding key insights. We used this successful group of sales professionals to then lead their peers over conference calls, mentoring, and in roundtable discussions. Intersecting personal gain and lasting legacy for the business can be a real motivator for your colleagues.

Enable Action by Removing Barriers:

As any organization grows, you will notice points of friction or difficult processes slowing down your team's work. In this stage you look for the bottlenecks in your team's work and for anything impeding customers from getting your product. How do you become a more accessible organization to work for and an easier one from which to buy?

For our launch, we wanted to bet on our product quality. We made some of our sales programs less restrictive and looked for easier ways to evaluate it with customer pilots. With barriers removed, we made it simpler for customers to obtain our product, and sales began ramping up...quickly.

Organizational politics can also hinder your efforts at this stage. All organizations have politics which can either help or interfere with your project. While a greater sense of purpose drives transcendent leaders, we can't ignore organizational politics which might slow down your progress. So, be aware of the politics and think practically about how to navigate them.

As Indra Nooyi, former Pepsi CEO, once said, "Understand the company's politics but don't play in the politics."

Generate Short-Term Wins:

Large change projects can take considerable time and effort to get off the ground. Often, we may not complete our work until months or years down the road. How do you keep the team focused and delay gratification until project completion? We need to make a major deal out of the (seemingly) minor wins!

As we learned about good habits in self-actualization, the same happens with organizational change. Little things add up over time. But how do you keep your team focused and motivated to do the little things? Maybe you could host celebrations for essential project milestones. Or a social media post celebrating your first, 100th, or 1,000th new customer. Or use visual metrics to track progress and success for your team.

Whatever you do, you need a cadence of short-term milestones and opportunities to celebrate with your team. After all, the root word of "momentum" is "moment." If you string together positive moments for your team, you are well on your way to accelerating change and driving momentum. Keep the mojo up!

For our launch, I created a launch dashboard to share our progress and success. Each month, we updated a wide constituency on our progress. Increases in procedures, new hospitals adopting the technology, positive social media posts from our customers, Wall Street analyst reports showcasing our product, you name it. We added anything that showcased momentum to the monthly dashboard. Afterwards, I made sure to send it to everyone vital to the launch, from our management board to all supporting function leaders and the selling organization. This *repetition* of wins and progress each month became exciting for the company. As success begets more success, our stakeholders now wanted to invest more into this product line and move even faster. We were off to the races.

Sustain Acceleration:

Planes use more energy to get off the ground during takeoff than they do the rest of the flight. And the same goes for change projects. You have to do a lot of work on the front end to get the plane in the air.

One big mistake large organizations take for granted is this need for acceleration. They will see some short-term wins on the board and assume the project is on its way to success, which couldn't be further from the truth. That's precisely when you need to double down and push the accelerators.

With our launch, we continued to look for ways to sustain adoption for the technology, seeing the hospital and patient care benefits. More physician partners wanted to work with us for research studies, continuing to showcase the benefits of this product in the clinical community. We also listened to customer feedback and made continual improvements to the product quality, enhancing their experience.

Too many times, large organizations will assume a project is headed in the right direction and begin putting its focus on something else. Please don't fall into this trap; finishing what you started is essential! How do you make sure you drive your success story to completion? Where attention goes, energy flows. Leaders need to keep their focus on successful projects to ensure they stay successful.

Institute Change: Make it Stick:

As this product launch began to hit the nine-figure mark, we began to clearly see this was a massive, transformative win for the company. More importantly, hospitals, physicians, and patients were benefitting around the world.

But, in a competitive healthcare environment, the moment you stop to rest, someone or something appears to replace you. With that in mind, we doubled down on this new technology with millions in R&D funds committed to future generations of this product line. The product's success actually spurred the vision for an entirely new platform, which many new products would be tied into. Similar to how Apple's iOS software makes the experience better for iCloud, iPhone, iPad, Apple TV, and the plethora of Apple devices in the market; we were creating a new ecosystem to create better outcomes for patients.

With your project riding high, make sure you recognize all the tireless work your team has done for the cause. How did their behaviors tie into the overall mission? This is where we create new systems and processes to ensure that new behaviors, mindsets, and working methods continue when team members disperse. If too much of the change's success lies only with the project leaders, your process won't stick. So how do we create a legacy of systems and processes to make your changes permanent?

There is an art and a science to driving change. The transcendent leader must master all these principles in order to leave a lasting legacy. If you are driven more by purpose over personal accomplishment, this is your time to shine.

Key Themes: Transcendence

⮩ Many view Adam Smith's *Wealth of Nations* as the launch of capitalism in the Western world. The original capitalists highly regarded the various stakeholders within their ecosystem, such as suppliers, customers, and the communities they serve.

⮩ University of Chicago professor Milton Friedman saw the stakeholder approach as limiting and felt that shareholder value was the primary pursuit for all businesses.

⮩ With numerous corporate scandals ushering in the 21st century, many business leaders have reconsidered the multi-stakeholder approach to business.

⮩ ESG (Environmental, Social, and Governance) goals aim to deliver financial results AND provide value to all stakeholders.

⮩ Customers should reward companies that deliver results for all stakeholders.

⮩ Driving change throughout the organization is a hallmark of transcendent leaders. Strong inspiration, motivation, and education is needed to bolster support for new ideas.

⮩ Former Harvard professor John Kotter's 8-step process has shown surprising durability in its effectiveness for organizational change in any era.

Maslow Magic: The Magic in the Application

➲ Who are all the stakeholders who touch your business? Are they all benefiting from your actions? What can you do to improve the outcomes for everyone engaged in your business, even for those who don't impact your financial results on the surface?

➲ What is a big change process your business desperately needs where you could use Kotter's 8-step framework? Who would you name as your guiding coalition and lieutenant army? Describe the before and after business conditions of this change project. What's holding you back?

CHAPTER 10

THE THEORY Z LEADER

"That job would drive me bonkers. It's loaded with bureaucracy, red-tape, and corporate politics. I want nothing to do with it. Plus, I really like my job now," said a close colleague who had elected not to interview for a big role leading an organization closing in on $1 billion in yearly sales. He was an early architect of our company, working with others to build an impressive streak of revenue and employee growth.

My colleague had recently endured a health scare, which resolved itself. Although physically healed, this scare had shifted his mental perspective on what was really important. He shunned the corporate rat race and only wanted to produce meaningful work. Although this job would have been a big promotion, he was content to let someone else get it.

As the weeks went on, top talent from around the company flooded in to interview for this role, a unique opportunity to lead a strong legacy business with a huge pipeline of new products. The gossip mill began to circulate even more on who was in the lead for the position.

One hard-charging, ambitious candidate from outside our business unit had emerged as a potential leader in the interview process. He had an impressive resume: former Division 1 athlete. MBA from an Ivy League school. Long track record with multiple leadership roles at large, established companies.

Despite the impressive resumes, one major gap was growing clear: the outside candidates seemed to lack an appreciation for the strong culture forged over twenty years, along with our deep commitment to the patient experience. It wasn't just what we had accomplished, but *how* we had built this growing engine that was inspiring. The culture was the X factor in delivering breakthrough innovation to patients around the world. Was it possible to lead this growing engine of the company without taking the time to appreciate its cultural strengths?

My colleague looked in the mirror and challenged himself. Was this just his ego talking? Or was it a genuine concern for the business and its people? After deep reflection, he realized it was a genuine concern for the business. My colleague threw his name into the ring to interview for the role and fight for its cultural values.

Theory Z

In the 1960s, an evolving thought process on the value of work in society appeared. Douglas McGregor, a management professor at the MIT Sloan School of Management, published the book *The Human Side of Enterprise*, which dives into this evolution.[142]

In his book, McGregor explains the phenomenon of Theory X and Theory Y motivations in the workplace. Theory X is an old-school, authoritarian style which assumes workers dislike their jobs and are lazy. They have little self-motivation and need strong direction from their superiors to get anything done.

Theory Y, on the other hand, aligns with Maslow's original hierarchy in the upper echelon of self-actualization. It assumes that workers don't need to be micromanaged, are self-directed, and eager to participate in decision-making.

Although McGregor and Maslow had mutual respect for each other, Maslow didn't feel that Theory Y was aligned with his expanded hierarchy and principle of transcendence. As a result, Maslow created Theory Z in his final years of life.

Theory Z applies to leaders who transcend the ego. "Maslow proposed that transcenders are metamotivated by higher ideals and values that go beyond the satisfaction of basic needs and the fulfillment of one's unique self," wrote Scott Barry Kaufman in *Transcend*.

Deborah Stephens and Gary Heil summed up the idea of Theory Z leadership in *Maslow on Management*. "The higher needs were reflected in job advertisements that noted friendly coworkers, pleasant surroundings, responsibility, freedom and autonomy, a chance to put one's ideas into action, a company of which one can be proud, a chance to make a difference."

They continued that "Theory Z presupposed that people, once having reached a level of economic security, would strive for a life steeped in values, a work life where the person could create and produce. Although Maslow died before finishing his work with Theory Z, we see evidence today that his theory was several decades ahead of its time."

Though Maslow never fully finished this idea of leadership in the workplace, it inspires us to see our work lives as a place for connection, creation, and fulfillment beyond ourselves.

Is Maslow's Summit Achievable?

Psychologist and author Scott Barry Kauffmann has extensively researched Maslow and his principles. Kauffmann notes that the ascent of Maslow's principles is a perpetual, enduring activity. "The process of becoming a person is an ongoing journey of discovery, openness, and courage, in which you reach higher and higher levels of integration and harmony within yourself and with the outside world, allowing greater flexibility and freedom to become who you truly want to become. Since you are always in a state of change, you are always in a state of becoming."[143]

As mentioned in this book's introduction, Maslow's Hierarchy and what it means to live a self-actualized life fascinated me as a college undergraduate. Through my research while writing this book, I learned that transcendence sits atop the summit of needs. But is it even possible to achieve the summit? Why do so few people operate in the upper echelon of Maslow's work? The work, after all, seems infinite.

An Infinite Game has Fuzzy Rules

So, what defines success on Maslow's spectrum of needs? When have we "made it"? Is it even clear what defines success?

Modern-day leaders are living in a fast-moving, ambiguous world where change is constant. Competitors come and go; customer needs change; employee motivation and values change. How can we even chart a course with all this disruption?

Author and Speaker Simon Sinek sought to answer those questions in his book, *The Infinite Game*, which illustrates two types of games in leadership: a finite game and an infinite game.[144]

Finite games have clear rules, a defined beginning and end, and apparent winners and losers. Fixed statistics, like market share, revenue, or stock price, can measure finite games. Since it seems so easy to define, many people do it. Finite leaders may define their careers by their job title, how much money they have, or even how many vacations they take in a year.

But with the world constantly changing, how sustainable is that? Infinite leaders, on the other hand, plan a different game. They recognize the rules are fuzzy, there's no way to define a win clearly, and players can immediately change how they play the game. Companies can emerge, thrive, struggle, and go bankrupt while the game goes on. Infinite leaders recognize the game never really ends. The goal shouldn't be to beat the competition but to *outlast* your competition.

Engaging in a fixed mindset can have disastrous consequences. Over-fixation with short-term metrics can cause you to cut the oxygen lifeline which sustains your business over the longer haul. A finite mindset focuses on the most urgent instead of the most important, setting up the company for eventual failure and breeding a culture of insecurity.

Finite companies may be more stable but are unprepared for massive disruption, whereas infinite game companies are designed to embrace unpredictable situations, adapt, and thrive in a fast-changing environment.

Principles of an Infinite Game

According to Sinek, infinite companies and leaders are built on five essential principles.

- ➲ Exist to further a just cause
- ➲ Build trust in their organization
- ➲ Establish worthy rivals
- ➲ Display existential flexibility to make massive shifts when necessary

➲ Have the courage to take the long-term view (infinite mindset) over the short-term

Sinek describes the principle of a "Just Cause," a purpose more significant than ourselves. How does your organization make the world a better place? You have much more sustainable motivation and direction when driven by purpose. Purpose provides the strength to outlast the inevitable challenges on your journey.

While short-term perks and incentives may produce short-term behavior, these perks can also create a mercenary culture. Instead, if your teams have bought into your purpose, you will develop highly motivated fans raving for the cause itself. Of course, short-term incentives aren't all bad, but they aren't sustainable in and of themselves.

Even outside of Sinek's observations, the link between purpose and performance grows quite clear. Wharton Professor Claudine Gartenberg studied organizational purpose with Columbia University and Harvard Business School researchers.[145] In that study, they evaluated 500,000 people across 429 firms over five years. The study observed companies with clear communication about their purpose had better operating and financial performance.

As we learned from Google's research on building effective teams, trust is critical to building a healthy team culture. Even the Navy Seals, which have some of the highest-performing soldiers in the world, utilize trust for their teams. If an individual is high on performance but low on trust, they won't have what it takes to become a Seal. Low-trust individuals focus on themselves and their accomplishments more than the team and the mission.

A worthy rival is something an infinite company or leader will look for to continuously improve. They don't shy away from competition; they embrace it. Infinite leaders recognize success isn't a fixed pie and more than one company and leader can "win." The pie grows bigger if multiple companies serve a noble purpose to advance a just cause. The Latin word for competition is *competere*, which means to "strive together." Even at its root, healthy competition can spur advancement and both parties improve. Competition should be sought after, not feared.

Lastly, infinite companies and leaders embrace existential flexibility to disrupt their business as the market changes. The business world is full of once-dominant companies unwilling to change when the game shifts.

Companies unwilling to be flexible are spread across business literature. Kodak wasn't willing to embrace the digital camera evolution and filed for bankruptcy in 2012. Streaming services like Netflix disrupted Blockbuster. Myspace was an early pioneer in social media but needed to bring the same user-friendly experience Facebook had. Toys R Us failed to innovate as e-commerce created more options for consumers and big box retailers like Wal-Mart and Target offered more. And who can forget Nokia, the global leader in mobile phones, who missed the shift to smartphones and lost their throne to Apple and Samsung?

Leaders and their organizations either get better or worse; they never stay the same. Those that establish a foundation of existential flexibility, purpose, and worthy rivals are built to outlast the inevitable winds of change.

The Second Mountain

Unfortunately, the pursuit of success doesn't always lead to deep-seated fulfillment at the end of your achievements; instead, it can lead to an empty, hollow sentiment. Despite receiving promotions, wealth, job titles, or status, achievements can still leave us with a feeling of emptiness. "Is this all there is?"

How did this happen? After all, we have checked off all the boxes of what conventional wisdom states will make us happy. So why don't our achievements resonate more when we accomplish what we set out to do? The world thinks I'm successful, but why don't I feel it?

David Brooks, an author and columnist for the *New York Times*, tried to understand this phenomenon better in his book *The Second Mountain*.[146] Brooks describes our journey through life in two mountains. The first mountain is what we foresee as a "successful" life, instilled in us from society, parental influences, conventional wisdom, etc. It includes how we achieve outer success, like job titles, wealth, and status. This is the mountain of worldly success.

The first mountain is all about individualism, widely celebrated in society today. What do I want to think, value, and do? How can I fully express my personal freedom? The prevailing societal thought is I should be able to do whatever I want as long as I'm not hurting anyone. After all, I don't want to hold back on appropriately "expressing myself."

Brooks points out the problems within chronic individualism. People talk to their neighbors less than they did in the past. Chronic loneliness has become an epidemic, per the U.S. Surgeon General. And the fastest-growing political and religious groups today are in the "unaffiliated" category. Political activity and our houses of worship were central places where we met, connected, and pursued a shared set of values, and this meaningful connection is no longer happening.

As individualism takes over and we lose our consistent social connections, we lose trust in society. We need faith in our institutions, government, companies, and neighbors to maintain our grounding.

As social connections deteriorate, people look more to their work to fill that gap. However, some take the same mindset of chronic individualism to their careers, continually let down by a lack of meaning. This individualism drives their desire to please their bosses, achieve higher levels of status and wealth, and always be moving forward.

The problem with this first mountain is we seek "happiness" as defined by the world, but this happiness doesn't endure in our souls. It can come with an event or a milestone but quickly dissipates into the day-to-day humdrum of life. Many high achievers haven't experienced enduring happiness, despite their outer "worldly success."

Brooks writes, however, that the second mountain focuses on a life of purpose and service for something greater than ourselves, which ultimately holds more meaning. This purposeful, service-driven life creates a vocation and not just a job. You are putting the needs of your families, teams, industry, and community above your own.

This second mountain can feel much larger than the first. Because it is. The second mountain's problems that affect a broader society can seem endless, contrary to many of the simpler challenges you might pursue based purely on chronic individualism. But the second mountain is much more meaningful. You know you made an impact and produced a legacy contributing to the well-being of other people and beloved institutions. You made a real, enduring difference.

While the first mountain may create momentary, fleeting happiness, the second mountain will produce a more enduring sense of fulfillment, meaning, and contribution.

Megatrends 2030

Now, more than ever, the world needs Theory Z leaders to expand our possibilities. To solve emerging problems. To tap into new solutions. To accelerate new opportunities. In the next decade, our challenges and opportunities will only increase.

A megatrend is a major movement or trend in the global environment, which disrupts the world today and tomorrow. They may be longer-term social, economic, environmental, political, or technological change. Blair Sheppard, PwC's Global leader of Strategy and

Leadership, discusses the emergence of megatrends.[147] "A decade ago, many people thought there was time to address the Megatrends in a leisurely way. But it has become obvious that is far from true. The Megatrends are coming at the world like a freight train, and they are creating more numerous and more acute crises, year after year. There's unlimited potential if humanity comes together to address the Megatrends, but we must act now."

With help from PwC, we identify the top five megatrends, which will have enormous stakes for government, organizations, and individuals. Transcendent Theory Z leaders must face these challenges to move our world forward.

Megatrend One: Climate Impact

The impact of human consumption on the environment has been well-documented, but how will this impact business leaders in the future? With rising temperatures and sea levels endangering coastal cities, and half of the world living under severe water stress, the climate will play a significant role in our future leader's decision-making.

Leaders must rethink how we can create a sustainable ecosystem with products and daily operations. Energy, water, and other critical raw materials are growing scarce, driving costs up. Floods, droughts, and storms all cause challenges to supply chains. A new era of job creation focused on green transformation will present an opportunity to improve our business outlook and elevate career paths.

Megatrend Two: Technology Disruption

Technology will continue to develop at a breakneck pace, accelerating most aspects of human life. From artificial intelligence, robotics, energy storage, DNA sequencing, blockchain technology and materials sciences, technology is outrunning human adaptability. If we refer back to Astro Teller's description of innovation outpacing human's capacity to learn, we almost need machines to help us manage the machines.

Despite its many advantages, rapid technology expansion exposes even more risks, such as cybersecurity issues, the spread of disinformation/misinformation, mental health issues, and job loss/insecurity. While technology dramatically enhances our production capabilities and complements our daily lives, it also blurs the boundary of what it means to be human.

Transcendent leaders will need to learn how to harness the power of technology but also curtail the risks associated with its vast speed of disruption. Leaders who don't digitally transform their organizations will be left obsolete. They also will need to expedite training and retraining for roles negatively impacted by technology. Lastly, the war for talent in STEM (Science, Technology, Engineering, Mathematics) will be greater than ever. Transcendent leaders must create an attractive work culture and career path options in order to tap into the necessary talent with the onslaught of new technology.

Megatrend Three: Demographic Shifts
While you need to watch for many demographic shifts over the coming decade, median age and population growth will be two of the most influential. With the median age increasing, the size of the workforce is shrinking relative to the greater population, which can manifest in many ways, and healthcare could see a big impact. With fewer providers and more patients, transcendent leaders will need to create efficient systems of care to address needs while not burning out the workforce. In countries with a younger median age, we see a population shift towards cities, leaving rural areas unmaintained. Changing ages will drive new consumption patterns, and businesses and governments must plan ahead.

The most significant societal impact of a rising median age is the fact we now have five generations in the workforce. From baby boomers, Generation X, millennials, and Generation Z, generational values and expectations are colliding. Transcendent leaders must create a purpose to inspire all work groups while harnessing the power of diverse thinking across demographics.

Megatrend Four: Nationalism Fracturing Diplomacy

With the fall of the Iron Curtain and the end to the Cold War, the U.S. led one of the most significant economic expansions in world history. The globalization of products and services lifted more people out of poverty than ever before, and the onslaught of open trade improved geopolitical relations. However, some countries feel the benefits of that expansion have been inequitable and want in on the action.

The new world order has competing spheres of interest, and countries quickly align with like-minded allies. The new order influencers will seek to impact with their political, economic, or societal model, while the destabilizers will seek to disrupt those gaining control.

The transcendent leader will need to seek allies who have a shared sense of values and are intimately connected with the local community. As we saw in the Russian invasion of Ukraine, leaders must confront the potential disruption of supply chains with rising political tensions worldwide. Leaders will face pressure to take a stand on specific issues. Theory Z leaders must transcend their ego to understand where to take a stand and when to comply with humility.

Megatrend Five: Social Instability

Disruption and the pace of change will constantly shake our global culture as growing disparities of money, power, and education will spread around the globe.. Those who can adapt will prosper; those who can't will struggle. Age will become an issue in most advanced countries as economies rush to handle an onslaught of needs. Polarization will continue to be a significant theme as people feel their governments are failing them.

The biggest challenge, however, is that of trust. Trust in institutions continues to decline, making governance and leadership more difficult. The world's problems cannot be solved without trust in our institutions. Theory Z leaders must show, not just tell, to develop trust. They must drive financial returns and long-term value for shareholders to fund the journey. Additionally, they need to inspire trust in all stakeholders, such as investing in their employees, dealing fairly with suppliers, driving sustainability throughout the business, and supporting the general well-being of their communities.

Trust is a precious asset: hard to obtain and easy to lose. However, Theory Z leaders who transcend their circumstances can drive a more prosperous and harmonious organization. Maslow described the importance of Trust in Love and Belonging. If we can develop trust on a global scale, humankind will flourish.

Leading with Authenticity and Inclusivity

Returning to the opening story of my colleague: with his deep belief in what we do for patients and people, my colleague went through the interview process and ultimately won the job of leading this large business unit. While the division's basic systems were in place and a solid product pipeline was in development, he realized we had one opportunity to strengthen our most precious asset: our culture.

The company's culture had always been a strength, serving both to attract and keep great talent. But, one thing was lacking. The outside world had become increasingly divisive with the political and social issues of the day, and fractures were growing in society. However, this leader wanted our business to be a haven for everyone to feel safe, seen, and connected to each other, regardless of personal belief systems. After all, we had more important work to do for patients and mankind than argue over petty differences.

My colleague led with an authentic, inclusive style, making everyone feel like they belonged, and the results followed. With a connected team from many backgrounds, he drove the business unit to a level never before seen. Even more impressive is the anonymous employee engagement surveys showed the highest satisfaction scores and lowest attrition rates in the company.

My colleague's authentic and inclusive style of leading developed greater trust and business results. And he served as an inspiring example to lead with genuine purpose. Theory Z leaders rise above their own needs for a cause greater than themselves, creating a ripple effect of goodwill.

Key Themes: The Theory Z Leader

- ➲ Social psychologist Conor McGregor proposed the Theory X and Theory Y leadership philosophies in the 1950s and 1960s. Theory X was an authoritarian management style, while Theory Y felt employees were motivated when they were involved in decision-making.
- ➲ Abraham Maslow thought Theories X and Y were limited and proposed a Theory Z management style. Individuals who transcended ego and pursued a calling above their personal interests embodied Theory Z leadership.
- ➲ Theory Z's work seems infinite. Leaders have existential flexibility and courageously take the long-term view.
- ➲ Strong Theory Z leaders build an inspiring sense of trust.

➲ Transcendent leaders pursue two mountains in their careers. The first mountain focuses on achievements based on personal interests. The second mountain focuses on a higher calling above their own needs.

➲ Theory Z leaders must tackle the significant megatrends of the next decade to lead their ecosystem of influence. Those trends include climate impact, technological disruption, demographic shifts, the rise of nationalism, and social instability.

Maslow's Magic: The Magic in the Application

➲ What higher purpose motivates you to transcend the ego and pursue something greater than yourself? How can this make a lasting impact in your business, your teams, and the world around you? What's holding you back from making this central in your leadership journey?

➲ For what do you want to be remembered? How will the world improve because you lived your purpose?

➲ What larger megatrend will have the most profound impact on your life and career?

➲ Now that you have written the above answers, in one or two sentences, what is your purpose?

CONCLUSION

You may be wondering if, after going deep through Maslow's journey, I'm currently sitting atop a mountain, in the lotus position, with a halo over my head. Or if I walk around radiating peace and charisma, turning everything I touch into gold. Or if every day is filled with boundless joy, meaning, and deep human connection? Well, sorry to disappoint but far from it.

To err is human, and I live an imperfect life like everyone else. I still lose my car keys too frequently (thank you AirTags!), and suffer from a distracted goldfish brain. I've made good hires and not-so-good hires. I've led successful projects and championed other ideas that ultimately failed. I've made inspiring statements and other times my words fell flat. I've lived a life of success and failure, probably just like you.

Through it all though, I have learned one thing I am good at: getting better. I'm obsessed with learning from the best, and Maslow's wisdom has profoundly impacted how I view human potential, for both myself and the world around me. His hierarchy provides an anchoring framework in times of great inspiration and when I fall off track. By operating at the intersection of psychological research, science, and leadership wisdom, our impact is limitless.

This wisdom is not for our own enjoyment; rather, it provides a roadmap to become the best version of ourselves, *so that we can bring out the best in others for a good cause.* That's the ultimate end game.

The Vitamin and the Tylenol

Leadership wisdom can sometimes feel like a vitamin and sometimes like a Tylenol. Vitamins are proactive measures to nourish us as we prepare for the road ahead, but Tylenol is much more reactive. We only reach for it in times of trouble. My hope is this book can be used in both ways. There are times when you may want to orient to its framework in your leadership journey. Or, reach for it in an 11th hour emergency as you're being pressed for decisions.

What started as a deep curiosity about the meaning of self-actualization created an introspective and expansive journey. Never in a million years did I think I would be writing a book, 25 years after that college course, about how to pull Maslow's theories together in a roadmap for achievement, fulfillment, and building a lasting impact.

Since we spend so much time in our careers, we have a unique opportunity to use them to create the best versions of ourselves and make a lasting impact on those around us.

In **Physiology**, we detailed the need for having a solid physical body and its impacts on our work. We learned through many examples how sleep, proper nutrition, and exercise can optimize our daily outcomes. In addition, we learned the risks to our career performance if we don't optimize our health.

In **Security**, we looked alternatively at building a "secure" career. Instead of conventional wisdom, where we try to lock into one career path, real security means having diverse skills to flex in various roles and industries. As problems become more complex and routine tasks are automated, we must look at issues from multiple angles.

In **Belonging**, we learned about the crisis of loneliness in today's world and how strong work teams can build the deep sense of connection we all crave. Being united with a group of individuals driven by the same purpose creates relationships where people feel safe and encouraged to confront challenging tasks.

We learned the value of managing the inner critic and the haters with **Esteem**. If we do great work, we are going to be criticized. Esteem is the launching pad for creativity; we must be vulnerable and put ourselves out there.

Despite conventional wisdom, Maslow argues that everyone should be considered **Creative**. We all have the creative tendencies to unlock innovation. When we build established frameworks like design thinking into our everyday practice, we can surprise ourselves with the opportunities we create for ourselves.

With **Aesthetics**, Maslow reminded us to see beauty and order in the world. We learned how grace, gratitude, and optimism can enhance our worldview. Mindfulness can be the vehicle to stop, be still, and recognize all that is present within us.

When those invested in **self-actualization** are firing on all cylinders, they have some of the best habit systems to make the right behaviors automatic, allowing them to focus and attend to what they love. Self-actualizers can lock into the "zone," or flow state, where they do their best and seek maximum fulfillment.

With **transcendence**, we recognize a complete life isn't just about building what's best for ourselves, but having a lasting impact on all stakeholders we encounter—leaving the world a little better than we found it.

Your Legacy

This career journey will be filled with twists, turns, detours, plateaus, and ascension. As we lean into these inevitable changes, we learn how our best selves can manifest in our careers.

Lastly, we need to extend our profound admiration for the work of Abraham Maslow. The psychology community criticized his early motivational theories but these same theories were embraced by the business world. His framework for motivation is timeless, and even after many decades still drives the path to achievement, fulfillment, and making a sound contribution to the world around us.

It's in our nature to seek out leadership wisdom in the modern buzzwords and social media platitudes. But the real answers don't always lie in what's new but in what's timeless. Maslow's work has provided the blueprint for successful living in any era. Abraham Maslow's transcendent impact on the world was made by showing us how to make our own.

ACKNOWLEDGEMENTS

As much as I wish this book was written from my talent alone, it'd be far from the truth. Through this process, I have truly felt God's presence in moments of inspiration, perseverance during writer's block, and introducing the right people at the exact right time. I just seemed to have the right assemblance of fellow writers, editors, publishers, illustrators, and prospective readers who came into this process at the perfect time to guide me on this journey. I am forever grateful.

First, I'd like to thank my wife, Lee, and my children, Jackson, Will, and Kate, for your inspiration and support throughout this process. You continue to motivate me to live a transcendent purpose and have given me the space to pursue the rabbit holes of my curiosity. I love you. I'd also like to thank my parents, Charles and Christine. Whatever my aspiration was—playing quarterback for my high school football team, pursuing a professional baseball dream, moving across the country to pursue career opportunities, or writing a book, your optimism and support has been everything. To my brother Derek, thank you for your friendship, humor, and advice throughout life's twists and turns. I cherish our connection.

There is no better example of "it takes a village" than supporting an author in their writing journey. Katie Desiderio, a colleague and friend, is the first person I told I was writing a book outside of my family. Her excitement, energy and mentorship motivated me as I struggled with bouts of imposter syndrome. Sandra Wendel was an extremely helpful resource as she assembled a team of fifteen beta readers to provide meaningful feedback in the early stages of a very raw manuscript. Katie Salisbury supported me during early-stage assessments and helped me fine tune my proposals.

My editing kicked into high gear when I met the Streamline Books leadership team, Alex Demczak and Will Severns. I love the mission Streamline is on to help authors find their voice, and it felt like the perfect fit for my first book. Thank you for the useful guidance, enthusiasm, and support on this journey. It made a major difference! Also, a big thank you needs to go to Jessica Burdg for diving into the manuscript with me to bring the stories to life. Jessica helped me take a book of academic principles and turn it into an engaging story. Her appreciation for my curiosity and enthusiasm for this unique view on leadership development gave me confidence throughout the journey. Lastly, Kiska Carr did a wonderful job in keeping the story flowing with a solid copy edit.

I am not in the least bit artistic and needed better talent around me for the illustrations on the book cover design and interior. Katie Fleming did a wonderful job with the book cover design, and showed extraordinary patience in my flip-flopping of choices and numerous revisions. Abigael Elliott did an amazing job with the illustrations in the book to help me bring old academic principles to life through images. Suzanna Lusk Chriscoe, thank you for the beautiful interior design that perfectly flowed with the illustrations and book themes. The finished product looks amazing.

I can't help but feel grateful for the inspiring leaders I have worked for throughout my career who have modeled transcendent leadership. I truly feel like I have won the lottery when considering the ecosystem of support through the twists and turns of my career. First, I want to thank Dan Lafond and Peter Prete for creating a fun and competitive environment to work in right out of college, fostering an enjoyment in my career for decades to come. Carrie Soroush, for believing in me at a time of career transition and giving me my first shot in medical sales. Ryan Casey, for challenging me to not settle on being average and to shoot for the stars.

Kristin LaRocca, thank you for your optimism and willingness to take new risks to explore what's around corners. Your early endorsement of my career has been instrumental in my journey. Chris Barron, for helping me build a disciplined approach to people leadership and business execution, many of those principles I still use today. Jerry Long, for bringing out my creative confidence and moving mountains to help me navigate undeveloped terrain for our business. Megan DiBella, for teaching me everything I know about product management, and being a great teammate and mentor during many big launches. Dave Cowell, thank you for modeling the way and showing how trust and inclusivity can be X factors in leading high-performing teams.

And lastly, I want to thank you, the readers. Thank you for investing your time into this journey, and I hope Maslow's insights can translate into your career and leadership impact. Our challenges and opportunities in today's world are unprecedented, and we need a transcendent leader now more than ever. I wish you well on your journey for a career of impact and helping make this world a better place.

AUTHOR BIOGRAPHY

As a NCAA Division 1 college athlete and team captain, Brian McGee was deeply motivated by the desire to drive healthy teamwork and optimal results. During his college experience, he became fascinated with Maslow's original hierarchy of needs, obsessed with understanding human potential and the intersection of peak fulfillment and achievement through the lens of Maslow's work.

Over the last twenty-five years, Brian has researched hundreds of topics in psychology, management science, and leadership wisdom. The first testing ground was applying these learnings to his own career journey; he then shared those findings with the various teams he's led. Having experience in both telecommunications and medical technology industries, Brian has spent his career at the forefront of the emerging tech landscape.

Today, Brian is a senior sales and marketing leader in the medical technology industry, an industry he has worked in for twenty years in seven different roles. His experience includes leading $150 million+ global product launches, driving organizational change, and being a highly sought-after mentor for career development. Brian has a thoughtful yet pragmatic style—keen for new ideas but always driven by results.

Brian earned a B.S. in Marketing from Seton Hall University and an MBA from Rutgers University. He lives in Charlotte, North Carolina, with his wife and three children. In his free time, he enjoys leading youth sports teams and helping the next generation become their best in body, mind, and spirit.

Brian would love to keep in touch with his readers. Please visit brianmcgee.net and sign up for the newsletter, where Brian looks forward to sharing more discussion on how psychological research, management science, and leadership wisdom can help the next generation of Theory Z leaders.

ENDNOTES

Introduction

1 Maslow, A. (1943). A theory of human motivation. *Psychological Review*, 370-396.

2 Akademiyesi, T. (2015, September 28). Tengritagh Akademiyesi. Retrieved July 27, 2023, from https://tengritagh.org/2015/09/28/abraham-harold-maslow-and-humanistic-theories-of-self-actualization/

3 *Humanistic Psychology (humanism).* (2018, March 8). Retrieved from GoodTherapy: https://www.goodtherapy.org/learn-about-therapy/types/humanistic-psychology

4 Pryce-Jones, J. (2010). *Happiness at Work-Maximizing Your Psychological Capital for Success.* Hoboken, NJ: Wiley.

5 Hoffman, E. (2008). Abraham Maslow: A biographer's reflections. *Journal of Humanistic Psychology*, 439-443.

6 Hoffman, E. (1988). *The Right to be Human: A Biography of Abraham Maslow.* New York: St. Martin's Press.

7 Boeree, C. G. (2006). *Personality Theories.* Retrieved from https://webspace.ship.edu/cgboer/maslow.html

Chapter 1

8 Sack, H. (2020, April 1). *Abraham Maslow and the Hierarchy of Needs.* Retrieved from SciHi Blog: http://scihi.org/abraham-maslow-hierarchy-needs/

9 Akademiyesi, T. (2015, September 28). *Tengritagh Akademiyesi.* Retrieved July 27, 2023, from https://tengritagh.org/2015/09/28/abraham-harold-maslow-and-humanistic-theories-of-self-actualization/

10 *Humanistic Psychology (humanism).* (2018, March 8). Retrieved from GoodTherapy: https://www.goodtherapy.org/learn-about-therapy/types/humanistic-psychology

11 Maslow, A. (1943). A theory of human motivation. *Psychological Review*, 370-396.

12 Kaufmann, S. B. (2019, April 23). *Who Created Maslow's Iconic Pyramid?* Retrieved from Scientific American: https://blogs.scientificamerican.com/beautiful-minds/who-created-maslows-iconic-pyramid/

13 Maslow, A. H. (1962). *Toward a psychology of being.* Princeton, N.J.: Van Nostrand.

14 Saeednia, M. (2010). Innovation in scheming Maslow's hierarchy of basic needs. *U.S.-China Education Review*, 94-100.

15 Maslow, A. H. (1970). *Motivation and Personality, Third Edition.* New York: Harper and Row Publishers, Inc..

16 Maslow, A. (1970). *Religions, Values, and Peak-Experiences.* New York: Penguin Group.

17 Conley, C. (2017). *Peak: How Great Companies Get Their Mojo from Maslow.* Hoboken: John Wiley and Sons.

18 Maslow, A. H. (1965). *Eupsychian Management: A Journal.* Richard D. Irwin Publishing.

19 Maslow, A. H. (1998). *Maslow on Management.* John Wiley & Sons, Inc.

20 Maslow, A. H. (2000). *The Maslow Business Reader.* John Wiley & Sons, Inc.

21 Conley, C. (2017). *Peak: How Great Companies Get Their Mojo from Maslow.* Hoboken: John Wiley and Sons.

22 Kaufmann, S. B. (2020). *Transcend: The New Science of Self-Actualization.* New York: TarcherPerigee.

23 Pryce-Jones, J. (2010). *Happiness at Work-Maximizing Your Psychological Capital for Success.* Hoboken, NJ: Wiley.

Chapter 2

24 Huffington, A. (2016). *The Sleep Revolution.* New York: Harmony Books. p.96

25 Huffington, A. (2016). *The Sleep Revolution.* New York: Harmony Books. p. 23.

26 Huffington, A. (2016). *The Sleep Revolution.* New York: Harmony Books. p. 265-267

27 Huffington, A. (2016). *The Sleep Revolution.* New York: Harmony Books. p. 245

28 USDA Economic Research Service. (2022). *Household Food Security in the United States in 2021.* USDA.

29 *Robert Wood Johnson Foundation.* (2023). Retrieved from State of Childhood Obesity: https://stateofchildhoodobesity.org/demographic-data/adult/

30 Tilley, C. (2024, March 1). *Daily Mail.* Retrieved from DailyMail.com: https://www.dailymail.co.uk/health/article-13145593/obesity-risk-global-health-hunger-america-worst-countries.html

31 *American Public Health Association.* (n.d.). Retrieved from apha.org: https://www.apha.org/~/media/files/pdf/factsheets/chronicdiseasefact_final.ashx

32 Spurlock, M. (Director). (2004). *Super Size Me* [Motion Picture].

33 Gonzalez, R. (2023). *Employee Nutrition-The Biting Impact on Your Bottom Line.* Retrieved from Corporate Wellness Magazine: https://www.corporatewellnessmagazine.com/article/the-biting-impact-of-employee-food-choices-on-your-bottom-line-2

34 Hollingshead, T. (2018). *Poor employee health means slacking on the job, business losses.* Retrieved from Brigham Young University

College of Life Sciences and Public Health: https://ph.byu.edu/
poor-employee-health-means-slacking-on-the-job-business-losses

35   *Food Labeling; Nutrition Labeling of Standard Menu Items
in Restaurants and Similar Retail Food Establishments.* (2014,
December 1). Retrieved from Federal Register: The Daily Journal
of the United States Government: https://www.federalregister.gov/
documents/2014/12/01/2014-27833/food-labeling-nutrition-labelin
g-of-standard-menu-items-in-restaurants-and-similar-retail-food

36   *Larger Portion Sizes Contribute to U.S. Obesity Problem.* (2013,
February 13). Retrieved from National Heart, Lung, and Blood
Institute: https://www.nhlbi.nih.gov/health/educational/wecan/
news-events/matte1.htm

37   Peterson, A. (2023, March 14). *The American Diet Has a
Sandwich Problem.* Retrieved from The Wall Street Journal: https://
www.wsj.com/articles/sandwich-american-diet-unhealthy-489a1d59

38   *Nearly 80 Percent of Working Americans Say They Don't
Drink Enough Water: Quench Survey.* (2018, June 19). Retrieved
from PR Newswire: https://www.prnewswire.com/news-releases/
nearly-80-percent-of-working-americans-say-they-dont-drink
-enough-water-quench-survey-300668537.html

39   Mayo Clinic Staff. (2022, October 12). *Nutrition and Healthy
Eating.* Retrieved from Mayo Clinic: https://www.mayoclinic.org/
healthy-lifestyle/nutrition-and-healthy-eating/in-depth/water/
art-20044256

40   *Spilling the Beans: How Much Caffeine is Too Much?* (2018,
December 12). Retrieved from U.S. Food and Drug Administration:
https://www.fda.gov/consumers/consumer-updates/spilling-bean
s-how-much-caffeine-too-much

41   Friedman, R. (2014, October 3). Regular Exercise Is Part
of Your Job. Retrieved from Harvard Business Review: https://hbr.
org/2014/10/regular-exercise-is-part-of-your-job

42   McKenna, J. (2008). Exercising at work and self-reported work performance. *International Journal of Workplace Health Management*, 176-197.

Chapter 3

43   Gallo, A. (2023, February 15). *What is Psychological Safety?* Retrieved from Harvard Business Review: https://hbr.org/2023/02/what-is-psychological-safety

44   Edmundson, A. (2024, October 23). Free Personal Psychological Safety Survey. Retrieved from Fearless Organization Scan: https://fearlessorganizationscan.com/engage/free-personal-psychological-safety-survey

45   *Number of Jobs, Labor Market Experience, Marital Status, and Health: Results from a National Longitudinal Study*. (2021, August 31). Retrieved from Bureau of Labor Statistics: https://www.bls.gov/news.release/pdf/nlsoy.pdf

46   Smith, A. (2012). *Wealth of Nations*. Ware, England: Wordsmith Editions.

47   Gladwell, M. (2008). *Outliers*. New York: Back Bay Books.

48   Friedman, T. L. (2016). *Thank You for Being Late*. New York: Farrer, Straus, and Giroux.

49   *Biography*. Retrieved from Astro Teller: http://www.astroteller.net/about/bio

50   Friedman, T. L. (2016). *Thank You for Being Late*. New York: Farrer, Straus, and Giroux.

51   Kosslyn, S. M. (2019, September 25). *Are You Developing Skills That Won't Be Automated*. Retrieved from Harvard Business Review: https://hbr.org/2019/09/are-you-developing-skills-that-won't-be-automated?registration=success

52   Sandberg, S. (2013). *Lean In: Women, Work, and the Will to Lead*. New York: Random House.

53 Epstein, D. (2019). *Range: Why Generalists Triumph in a Specialized World.* New York: Riverhead Books.

54 Epstein, D. (2019). *Range: Why Generalists Triumph in a Specialized World.* New York: Riverhead Books.

55 Gullich, A., Macnamara, B. N., & Z., H. D. (2021). What Makes a Champion? Early Multidisciplinary Practice, Not Early Specialization, Predicts World-Class Performance. *Perspectives on Psychological Science,* 1-24.

56 Chandy, R. (2017, April 24). *So hire me: how diversity of experience adds value.* Retrieved from London Business School: https://www.london.edu/think/so-hire-me-how-diverse-experience s-increase-professional-value

57 Cram, P., Anderson, M. L., & Shaughnessy, E. E. (2020). All Hands on Deck: Learning to "Un-specialize" in the COVID-19 Pandemic. *Journal of Hospital Medicine,* 314-315.

58 Chandy, R. (2017, April 24). *So hire me: how diversity of experience adds value.* Retrieved from London Business School: https://www.london.edu/think/so-hire-me-how-diverse-experience s-increase-professional-value

59 Blakely, S. (n.d.). *Sara Blakely.* Retrieved from LinkedIn: https://www.linkedin.com/posts/sarablakely27_success-entrepreneu r-activity-7059183172009291777-a4YI/?trk=public_profile_like_view

Chapter 4

60 Maslow, A. (1943). A Theory of Human Motivation. *Psychological Review,* 370-396.

61 Goldsmith, M., & Reiter, M. (2007). *What got you here won't get you there: how successful people become even more successful.* New York: Hyperion.

62 *Workplace Culture: What It Is, Why It Matters, and How to Define It.* (2019, February 1). Retrieved from ERC: Making Workplaces

Great: https://yourerc.com/blog/post/workplace-culture-what-it-is-wh
y-it-matters-how-to-define-it

63   Schwantes, M. (2019, March 27). *Warren Buffett Says He Became a Self-Made Billionaire Because He Played by 1 Simple Rule of Life (Which Most People Don't)*. Retrieved from Inc.: https:// www.inc.com/marcel-schwantes/warren-buffett-says-he-became-a-self-made-billionaire-because-he-played-by-1-simple-rule-o f-life-which-most-people-dont.html

64   Duckworth, A. (2016). *Grit: The Power of Passion and Perseverance*. New York: Scribner.

65   Clynes, T. (2015, June 13). *The "rage to master": What it takes for those scary-smart kids to succeed*. Retrieved from Salon: https:// www.salon.com/2015/06/13/talent_practice_luck_all_of_the_above_ what_it_takes_for_the_gifted_child_to_succeed/

66   Gladwell, M. (2008). *Outliers*. New York: Back Bay Books.

67   Ericsson, K., Tesch-Roemer, C., & Krampe, R. T. (1993). The Role of Deliberate Practice in the Acquisition of Expert Performance. *Psychological Review*, 363-406.

68   Tuckman, B. W. (1965). Developmental sequence in small groups. *Psychological Bulletin*, 384-399.

69   *Learn about Google's manager research*. (2023, August 1). Retrieved from re:Work: https://rework.withgoogle.com/guides/ managers-identify-what-makes-a-great-manager/steps/learn-abou t-googles-manager-research/

70   Rozovsky, J. (2015, November 17). *The five keys to a successful Google team*. Retrieved from re:Work: https://rework.withgoogle.com/ blog/five-keys-to-a-successful-google-team/

Chapter 5

71   *Stuart Smalley*. (2023, April 4). Retrieved from Wikipedia: https://en.wikipedia.org/wiki/Stuart_Smalley

72 Maslow, A. (1943). A Theory of Human Motivation. *Psychological Review*, 370-396.

73 McCarthy, E. (2015, April 23). *Roosevelt's "The Man in the Arena"*. Retrieved from Mental Floss: https://www.mentalfloss.com/article/63389/roosevelts-man-arena

74 *About Brené*. (2023). Retrieved from Brené Brown: https://brenebrown.com/about/

75 Brown, B. (2012). *Listening to shame*. Retrieved from Ted: https://www.ted.com/talks/brene_brown_listening_to_shame?language=en

76 Clance, P., & Imes, S. (1978). The imposter phenomenon in high achieving women: Dynamics and therapeutic intervention. *Psychotherapy: Theory, Research & Practice*, 241-247.

77 Dweck, C. S. (2016). *Mindset: The New Psychology of Success*. New York: Random House.

78 Gervais, M. *242: The Fleeting Nature of Flow State*. Retrieved from Finding Mastery Podcast: https://findingmastery.com/podcasts/becky-sauerbrunn/

79 *Kara Lawson: Handle Hard Better*. (2022). Retrieved from YouTube: https://www.youtube.com/watch?v=oDzfZOfNki4

80 *The playbook-Doc Rivers Rule #4: "Pressure is a Privilege!"*. (2021). Retrieved from YouTube: https://www.youtube.com/watch?v=nnnO8oO7Q9I

81 Gervais, M. (2019, May 2). *How to Stop Worrying About What Other People Think of You*. Retrieved from Harvard Business Review: https://hbr.org/2019/05/how-to-stop-worrying-about-what-other-people-think-of-you

82 *About Tim Ferris*. (2023). Retrieved from tim.blog: https://tim.blog/about/

83 *Tim Ferriss: 7 Great Principles for Dealing with Haters*. (2010, April 29). Retrieved from Mashable: https://mashable.com/archive/deal-with-haters-tim-ferriss

84   Temin, D. (19, November 2010). *The Sociopath In The Office Next Door*. Retrieved from Forbes: https://www.forbes.com/2010/11/19/sociopath-boss-work-forbes-woman-leadership-office-evil.html?sh=5e8376962a25

85   Urban, T. (2014, June 13). *Taming the Mammoth: Why You Should Stop Caring What Other People Think*. Retrieved from Wait But Why: https://waitbutwhy.com/2014/06/taming-mammoth-let-people s-opinions-run-life.html

Chapter 6

86   Kelley, T., & Kelley, D. (2013). *Creative Confidence*. New York: Crown Business.

87   Maslow, A. H. (2000). *The Maslow Business Reader*. John Wiley & Sons, Inc.

88   Coleman, J. (2012, August 15). *For Those Who Want to Lead, Read*. Retrieved from Harvard Business Review: https://hbr.org/2012/08/for-those-who-want-to-lead-rea

89   Taylor, K. (2017, August 22). *Five Mistaken Assumptions Business People Have about Creativity and Innovation*. Retrieved from Evergreen Leadership: https://evergreenleadership.com/2017/08/22/creativity-an d-innovation-five-mistaken-assumptions/

90   Rittel, H., & Webber, M. (1973). Dilemmas in a General Theory of Planning. *Policy Sciences*, 155-169.

91   *Hello, I'm David Kelley*. (2023). Retrieved from Ideo: https://www.ideo.com/people/david-kelley

92   Kelley, T., & Kelley, D. (2013). *Creative Confidence*. New York: Crown Business.

93   Mindful Marks. (2018, June 9). *1. Design Thinking: Empathize*. Retrieved from YouTube: https://www.youtube.com/watch?v=q654-kmF3Pc

94   Kortina, A. (2014, June 9). *Origins of Venmo*. Retrieved from Kortina.nyc: https://kortina.nyc/essays/origins-of-venmo/

95   Mindful Marks. (2018, June 9). *3. Design Thinking: Ideate*. Retrieved from YouTube: https://www.youtube.com/watch?v=zbLxs6te5to

96   Kiner, D. (2021, February 1). *Chick-fil-A manager fixes backlogged COVID-19 vaccine drive-thru: report*. Retrieved from Penn Live : https://www.pennlive.com/food/2021/02/chick-fil-a-manager-fixes-backlogged-covid-19-vaccine-drive-thru-report.html

97   Mindful Marks. (2018, June 9). *4. Design Thinking: Prototype*. Retrieved from YouTube: https://www.youtube.com/watch?v=Q4MzT2MEDHA

98   Ries, E. (2017). *The Startup Way: How modern companies use entrepreneurial management to transform culture and drive long-term growth*. New York: Currency.

99   Kindergan. (2017, October 31). *Digital Magic: How Eric Ries Brought The Startup Way to GE*. Retrieved from GE: https://www.ge.com/news/reports/digital-magic-eric-ries-brought-startup-way-ge

100   Mindful Marks. (2018, June 10). *5. Design Thinking: Test*. Retrieved from YouTube: https://www.youtube.com/watch?v=UVEQCNM6X-A

101   Team Mighty, We Are The Mighty. (2015, December 21). *11 quotes that show the great leadership of General George Patton*. Retrieved from Business Insider: https://www.businessinsider.com/11-quotes-that-show-the-great-leadership-of-general-george-patton-2015-11

102   Rogers, E. M. (1962). *Diffusion of innovations*. New York: Free Press of Glencoe.

103   Benna, S. (2015, July 22). *This billion-dollar company failed 39 times before becoming successful*. Retrieved from Business Insider: https://www.businessinsider.com/wd-40-failed-39-times-before-becoming-successful-2015-7

104   Utley, J. (2013, March 21). *How to overcome a lack of buy-in for design thinking*. Retrieved from YouTube: https://www.youtube.com/watch?v=gZSIG5nj93U

Chapter 7

105 Robbins, T. (2023). *Understanding the Gift of Grace.* Retrieved from Tony Robbins: https://www.tonyrobbins.com/the-gifts-of-life/grace

106 Daily Stoic. (2021). *Amor Fati: The Formula for Human Greatness.* Retrieved from Daily Stoic: https://dailystoic.com/amor-fati-love-of-fate/

107 Jocko Podcast. (2016, January 25). *Jocko Willink "Good" (Official).* Retrieved from YouTube: https://www.youtube.com/watch?v=IdTMDpizis8

108 *Marcus Tullius Cicero > Quotes > Cicero.* (2023). Retrieved from Goodreads: https://www.goodreads.com/quotes/72368-gratitude-is-not-only-the-greatest-of-virtues-but-the

109 McCullough, M., Emmons, R., & Tsang, J. (2002). The grateful disposition: A conceptual and empirical topography. *Journal of Personality and Social Psychology*, 112-127.

110 Gervais, M., & Carroll, P. (2020). *Compete to Create [AudioBook].* Audible Originals.

111 Seligman, M. E. (1991). *Learned Optimism.* New York: A.A. Knopf.

112 Mind Tools Content Team. (2023). *The ABC Model.* Retrieved from Mind Tools: https://www.mindtools.com/arh8314/the-abc-model

113 Mindful Staff. (2017, February 9). *Finding Mastery: A Conversation with Michael Gervais and Jewel .* Retrieved from Mindful: https://www.mindful.org/finding-mastery-michael-gervais-jewel/

114 *Colin L. Powell's Thirteen Rules of Leadership.* (2021, October 18). Retrieved from U.S. Department of State: https://www.state.gov/dipnote-u-s-department-of-state-official-blog/colin-l-powells-thirteen-rules-of-leadership/

115 Jackson, P., & Delehanty, H. (1995). *Sacred Hoops: Spiritual Lessons of a Hardwood Warrior.* New York: Hyperion.

116   Gervais, M., & Carroll, P. (2020). *Compete to Create [AudioBook]*. Audible Originals.

117   Bandelow, B., & Michaelis, S. (2015). Epidemiology of anxiety disorders in the 21st century. *Dialogues in Clinical Neuroscience*, 327-335.

118   Killingsworth, M. A., & Gilbert, D. T. (2010). A wandering mind is an unhappy mind. *Science*, 932.

119   *About Jon Kabat-Zinn*. (2023). Retrieved from Jon Kabat-Zinn: https://jonkabat-zinn.com/about/jon-kabat-zinn/

120   Kabat-Zinn, J. (2005). *Wherever You Go, There You Are*. New York: Hyperion.121   Frankl, V. E. (1962). *Man's Search for Meaning: An Introduction to Logotherapy*. Boston: Beacon Press.

122   Ferriss, T. (2017). *Tribe of Mentors: Short Life Advice from the Best in the World*. New York: Harper Business.

123   Gervais, M., & Carroll, P. (2020). *Compete to Create [AudioBook]*. Audible Originals.

124   Basso, J. C., McHale, A., Ende, V., Oberlin, D. J., & Suzuki, W. A. (2019). Brief, daily meditation enhances attention, memory, mood, and emotional regulation in non-experienced meditators. *Behavioural Brain Research*, 208-220.

125   Wozniak, M. (2020). *50 Famous People Who Meditate*. Retrieved from Meditation Wise: https://www.meditationwise.com/50-famous-people-who-meditate

126   La Roche, J. (12, February 2014). *How Meditation Makes Ray Dalio Feel 'Like a Ninja In A Fight'*. Retrieved from Business Insider: https://www.businessinsider.com/ray-dalio-2014-2

Chapter 8
127   Maslow, A. (1943). A Theory of Human Motivation. *Psychological Review*, 370-396.

128   Clear, J. (2018). *Atomic habits: Tiny changes, Remarkable Results; An Easy And Proven Way to Build Good Habits and Break Bad Ones.* New York: Avery, an imprint of Penguin Random House.

129   Csikszentmihalyi, M. (1990). *Flow: The Psychology of Optimal Experience.* New York: Harper and Row.

130   Sawyer, K. (2007). *Group genius: The creative power of collaboration.* New York: Basic Books.

131   Kotler, S. (2020). *Frequently Asked Questions On Flow.* Retrieved from Steven Kotler: https://www.stevenkotler.com/rabbit-hole/frequently-asked-questions-on-flow

132   Yerkes, R., & Dodson, J. (1908). The relation of strength of stimulus to rapidity of habit-formation. *Journal of Comparative Neurology and Psychology*, 459-482.

133   Maslow, A. H. (1971). *The farther reaches of human nature.* New York: Viking Press.

Chapter 9

134   Kaufmann, S. B. (2020). *Transcend: The New Science of Self-Actualization.* New York: TarcherPerigee.

135   Collins, J. (2001). *Good to Great.* London: Random House Business Books.

136   Collins, J. (n.d.). *Level 5 Leadership.* Retrieved from Jim Collins: https://www.jimcollins.com/concepts/level-five-leadership.html

137   Venter, H. J. (2012). Maslow's Self-Transcendence: How It Can Enrich Organization Culture and Leadership. *International Journal of Business, Humanities and Technology*, 64-71.

138   Smith, A. (2012). *Wealth of Nations.* Ware, England: Wordsmith Editions.

139   Friedman, M. (1970, September 13). The Social Responsibility of Business is to Increase its Profits. *The New York Times.*

140   Chesto, J. (2017, October 5). Firm behind 'Fearless Girl' statue to pay $5m over equal pay for women, minorities. Retrieved from Boston Globe: https://www.bostonglobe.com/business/2017/10/05/state-street-boston-based-firm-behind-fearless-girl-statue-pay-case-alleging-pay-discrimination-against-women-minorities/ZJoCFfgrUrWDb9bNTdrcRN/story.html

Chapter 10

141   Kotter, J.P. (1996). Leading Change. Boston: Harvard Business School Press.

142   McGregor, D. (1960). *The Human Side of Enterprise*. New York: McGraw-Hill.

143   Kaufmann, S. B. (2020). *Transcend: The New Science of Self-Actualization*. New York: TarcherPerigee.

144   Sinek, S. (2019). *The Infinite Game*. New York: Portfolio/Penguin.

145   Gartenberg, C., Prat, A., & Serafeim, G. (2019). Corporate Purpose and Financial Performance. *Organization Science*, 1-18.

146   Brooks, D. (2019). *The Second Mountain: The Quest for a Moral Life*. New York: Random House.

147   PwC. (2023). *Megatrends: Five global shifts reshaping the world we live in*. Retrieved from PwC: https://www.pwc.com/gx/en/issues/megatrends.html